ISBN 0-87666-895-3

Photo Credits:
William Groody: pp. 41, 43, 53, 56, 57, 131, 140, 142, 148, 150, 187 (top), 191, 198, 231, 238, 243, 270, 273, 274; Mark Miller: 83, 101, 187 (bottom), 208, 209, 221, 258; Paul Hunter: pp. 108, 111, 114, 116; Donald LaConte: pp. 87, 91; Tom Dover: p. 90; Raphael S. Gadbois: p. 10; Harold A. Hurlbutt: pp. 14, 16; Debbie Smith: p. 86; Phil Frisk: pp. 23, 119; Harry V. Lacey: pp. 12, 15, 20, 36, 46, 58, 64, 69, 72 (bottom), 124, 132, 146, 189 (top), 190 (top and bottom left), 192, 195, 215, 216, 282; Dr. Herbert R. Axelrod: pp. 18, 73, 76, 77, 96, 278; Horst Bielfeld: pp. 26, 135, 152, 157, 200, 232, 262, 271; Louise Van der Meid: 28, 172 (bottom), 173 (bottom), 176 (bottom), 224; Three Lions: title page and pp. 31, 169 (top), 172 (top), 173 (top), 176 (top), 225; Dr. Gerald E. Allen: pp. 65, 84; San Diego Zoo: pp. 6, 80, 89; Courtesy of Vogelpark Walsrode: pp. 44, 48, 51, 72 (top), 145, 159, 168 (top), 180 (bottom), 184 (top), 185, 190 (bottom right), 228, 236 (bottom), 240 (top), 248 (top); Ken Stepnell: pp. 81, 85, 237; Harald Schultz: p. 88; Cliff Bickford: p. 92; Dr. John Moore: p. 93; John Warham: p. 137; New York Zoological Society: p. 154; Vince Serbin: p. 188; A. Young: p. 161 (bottom); G. Churchett: p. 161 (top); Keith Hindwood: pp. 165, 240 (bottom); H. Wright: p. 168 (bottom); Irene and Michael Marcombe: p. 189 (bottom); R. Good: p. 256; H. Schrempf: pp. 233, 253; A. J. Moff: p. 236 (top); D. R. Baylis: p. 241; P. Leysen: p. 275.

Distributed in the U.S. by T.F.H. Publications, Inc., 211 West Sylvania Avenue, PO Box 427, Neptune, NJ 07753; in England by T.F.H. (Gt. Britain) Ltd., 13 Nutley Lane, Reigate, Surrey; in Canada to the pet trade by Rolf C. Hagen Ltd., 3225 Sartelon Street, Montreal 382, Quebec; in Southeast Asia by Y.W. Ong, 9 Lorong 36 Geylang, Singapore 14; in Australia and the South Pacific by Pet Imports Pty. Ltd., P.O. Box 149, Brookvale 2100, N.S.W. Australia; in South Africa by Valid Agencies, P.O. Box 51901, Randburg 2125 South Africa. Published by T.F.H. Publications, Inc., Ltd, the British Crown Colony of Hong Kong.

Adventures with Talking Birds

Catherine Hurlbutt

Cockatoos are much in demand as pet birds, but their great popularity does not stem from their ability to talk.

TABLE OF CONTENTS

Dedication
To my mother, a successful
schoolteacher in her youth, and
the first member of her family
to teach a bird to talk.

ACKNOWLEDGMENTS

I wish to acknowledge the assistance of the National Geographic Society, Washington, DC, the U.S. Fish and Wildlife Service, Patuxent, Maryland, the Zoological Society of San Diego, the Zoological Society of London, England, and the Zoological Board of Victoria, Australia, which replied to technical queries; Mr. William R. Ganey of San Francisco whose extraordinary knowledge of published literature on talking birds enabled me to locate obscure but valuable reference material; and David L. Goodman, Lulita Pritchett, Donald and Hazel Thatcher, Lillian Theiling, and Harold Webster, who read the manuscript and offered constructive criticism. I am also indebted to many bird clubs and private individuals who shared experiences with me that greatly broadened the scope of this book.

All of the drawings are by Joseph C. Rigli.

African grey parrots are better known for their talking ability than their beauty.

Foreword

At some time in every person's life events occur that bring about permanent changes in lifestyles, and the incidents that resulted in my undertaking a study of talking birds were a turning point in my own life. The record of my activities during the years following that turning point is set forth in this book. I do not claim to have written THE definitive book on talking birds. The final word can never be written on any facet of animal behavior, because, like human beings, every specimen of the more intelligent animals is an individual. I emphasize that what I have written relates only to the way my individual birds performed under the influence of my personality and in the environment in which they lived. Though they remained healthy on the diets and the care which I have set forth, another researcher might achieve entirely different and even more productive results working with other individual birds and using different training and feeding regimens. It is my hope that by relating my experience to the welfare of either mankind or the subjects under study, this kind of research contributes to the sum of human knowledge and broadens man's understanding of his fellow creatures.

CHAPTER I

Hooked on Talking Birds

"How come you already had a cage out here to put that bird in?" queried a puzzled engineer as he met me coming down a hall in our office building with my prize—an escaped parakeet—in a cage, after a chase from the fourteenth to the fourth floor had attracted the attention of half the office force.

"Oh, no one ever knows when he might need a bird cage," I replied airily. "I always carry one in the car."

This was not the first time I had astonished people with my birding activities. Anyone who attempts to follow the devious paths of Nature's creatures is bound to attract some attention if he continues his observations long enough, and I had been following birds for a long time. They had always fascinated me. One of my earliest recollections is of being stuck in a vast jungle near my childhood home in northern Wyoming. I had crawled into that wilderness to reach a bird's nest I had spotted from the outside. Since there are no redwood groves in Wyoming, in retrospect I suppose I was actually caught in one of the brush thickets that dot the foothills of the Big Horn Mountains.

My interest in birds continued through my adolescence on our ranch in Colorado, but after entering Uncle Sam's labor force as a stenographer, I was confined to a city environment for many years. My nature activities consisted mainly of attending bird club meetings and writing letters to the editors, denouncing attitudes I considered inimical to wildlife.

Then one day a fellow employee brought into the office a baby female parakeet named Mikki, the first product of his

Bluebell and Dandy—my first "cage" birds.

new avocation—raising Australian budgies. As Mikki's little toes tightened around my finger I suddenly felt a long-slumbering spirit within me awaken, and I realized I must re-establish my associations with live birds. In due course Mikki's parents presented her with a brother and a sister, one blue and one green. I promptly purchased them, named them Bluebell and Dandy, and from that time on my life was never again to be birdless.

At the time I acquired Bluebell and Dandy, the Australian shell (or grass) parakeet, commonly called "budgie," was popularly known as the lovebird and always kept in pairs, under the erroneous assumption that a single parakeet would die of loneliness. With companionship of their own kind, of course, the birds did not talk, and their ability to mimic the human voice was not generally recognized. However, by the time Bluebell and Dandy had lived out their allotted spans, budgies had come into their own as talkers; and when I purchased a chartreuse male parakeet which I named Frisky, I resolved that I would train him to talk.

At first Frisky fully met my expectations. Within a few weeks he was saying "I'm cute" and giving the wolf whistle, but then followed a long period with no new words added. I complained to my mother, who lived with me, that if parakeets take so long to learn a new phrase it is no wonder that most of them say little more than "Pretty bird" or "Give me a kiss."

Not long after, when I came home from work one evening, my mother remarked encouragingly, "I don't think you need to worry about Frisky not learning any more. Today he said 'Are you a happy boy?' You know—like we say it."

Her use of the pronoun "we" was entirely in deference to my own feelings. I had never even thought of saying that phrase. Nevertheless, that evening I heard Frisky say something that sounded like it, and his rendition over the next few days improved with practice. Puzzled at this turn of events, I asked my mother what she and Frisky did during my absence.

She replied that she opened and closed the venetian blinds at Frisky's window several times a day and that recently he had shown considerable interest in this operation, clinging to her side of the cage as long as she was near. Her response to these friendly overtures had been to say to him, "Are you a happy boy?"

I did some heavy thinking about this unexpected insight into Frisky's learning processes. It took no Sherlock Holmes to deduce that the problem lay not in his mental capacity but in his choice of a teacher. When I told my mother it was obvious Frisky had switched from me to her as his model, she brushed the suggestion aside as absurd. I then persuaded her to enter a contest with me. I would say "Polly want a cracker?" to Frisky as often as I could, and she was to say "Where's Armelia?" (her name) whenever she thought of it. "Polly want a cracker" never got off the ground, but Frisky was soon saying "Where's Armelia?" repeatedly. Finally convinced that if there was to be a talking bird in the house she would have to be the educator, and amused at my comment that after a lapse of sixty years

Budgies are well known as birds which can develop extensive vocabularies.

she was again resuming her role as a school teacher, my mother took up Frisky's training in earnest. Before long he was saying his name and address and "I like Catherine Hurlbutt." When I first heard him say the latter, I realized she had rehearsed him in it secretly to salve my wounded ego. His actions, however, belied these words, and the fact that he said them so readily substantiated the opinion of most bird experts that "talking" birds do not understand the words they say. As if to purge himself of all remnants of his former association with me, he even abandoned the wolf whistle, which he had rendered excellently but which my mother could not—or would not—produce. But, thanks to her efforts, he did acquire an interesting repertoire. My humiliation over his rejection was replaced by amusement at my mother's expression of quiet self-satisfaction toward visitors who remarked that if they were around, they would teach the bird some salty language. On such occasions I would tell them their efforts would be useless—my mother alone determined what Frisky would say.

Then, when he was only two and a half years old, Frisky developed a tumor on his chest and, in spite of treatment by

My mother with Frisky, my first "talking" bird.

two veterinarians, died shortly thereafter. "He was a wonderful little bird and we didn't have him very long," was my mother's tight-lipped eulogy as I removed the pathetic little corpse.

My efforts to replace Frisky with another talker met with little success for some months. Then, on an impulse, I went into a pet shop operated by a lively little widow named Anna Curtis, who was to have a considerable influence on my later experiments with talking birds. She brought out an unprepossessing little blue budgie with frizzled wing and tail feathers, stating she was certain I would not be disappointed in him. "He's a good bird," she said. "I know what the parents are."

However, there was never to be another Frisky in our family. The new bird liked everybody and would imitate anyone who paid attention to him. But even if he had been disposed to be a "one-man" bird, my mother, by then, was no longer capable of the physical and mental effort necessary to develop a talking bird. When a few years later she herself walked through the Heavenly Portals, I like to think that a little chartreuse parakeet which had been flying around the celestial parks and gardens saying "Where's Armelia?" alighted on her shoulder and announced, "I'm a happy boy."

Yet, if my mother had not lost her little pet, a fascinating path for my own future activities might never have developed—for the disheveled little blue bird I purchased for another try developed into the famous Frosty, who amazed all who heard him with his rendition of the names of all fifty states and their state birds, as well as many complicated phrases.

However, Frosty himself died at an early age, killed Halloween night when he broke his neck in a loop of wire I had carelessly overlooked in his cage. I was heartbroken, of course, and my plans for a series of bird programs featuring Frosty in the role of "announcer" died with him; unknown

17

It was once believed that lovebirds, like budgies, had to be kept in pairs so that the birds would not die.

to me, however, the event helped shape my own destiny. My experience with Frisky and Frosty had made me realize that I could never again be satisfied without a talking bird. Thus, when further attempts with parakeets did not produce another winner, I turned in desperation to another group of "talking birds"—the mynahs. True to the reputation of his species, my first mynah, Snowball, talked, but he did not "use" my voice. Instead, he imitated that of my neighbor Mrs. Ham, whom I shall introduce in the next chapter. My frustration was mounting but so was a more constructive emotion—wonder. Why do birds talk at all? Why do some species talk and others not? How does one develop the ability in those that do? and so on. To get first-hand information on this phenomenon, I set for myself the goal of acquiring a member of each species known to imitate the human voice. After the mynah came the magpies, Mr. and Miss America, then Mortimer the starling, Henry the crow, Sammy Bluejay, as many of the parrots as I could afford, and finally the mighty raven, Edgar.

On the fifth anniversary of Frosty's death, I closed the door on the last contingent of little goblins and, while nibbling on the leftover trick-or-treat handouts, I reflected on my present and future status. Ahead of me lay the conditions that face anyone at my time of life: old age, increasing health problems, loneliness—all regarded as arch enemies of a satisfying life. Yet, thanks to the avenue opened up by my short-lived little pets, any of these liabilities, in my particular case, could be assets, since each of them would provide me with that ingredient essential in making a study of any form of wildlife—plenty of leisure. An absorbing interest in the present and an incentive for the future—this was the legacy that Frisky and Frosty had left me. As I prepared Snowball's paper "bedroll" and placed him in it, I realized that I had witnessed a demonstration of the philosophy that "all things work together for good" and that there is a purpose behind even the fall of a sparrow.

Even magpies could be charmed by Mrs. Ham.

20

CHAPTER II
Friendly Rivals

Back in the "Good Old Days" of BTV (Before Television), when radio was the popular form of home entertainment, I enjoyed the "live" broadcasts of the U.S. Army, Navy, and Marine Bands with their renditions of brass ensembles and solos. One trumpet trio featured periodically was titled "Friendly Rivals." With my primitive tape recorder I recorded this selection off the radio for my future listening pleasure, never dreaming that it would become my theme song in a project which, at that time, I never suspected I would undertake.

Rivalry, I was to learn, can be very frustrating, especially friendly rivalry, in which cordial attitudes throw victims off guard and allay all suspicions. But rivalry also can be very stimulating; it presents a challenge which calls forth the best efforts of competitors and thus is an excellent teacher. In this way I was to learn a lot about birds, myself, and human personality and capabilities which otherwise I would not have known.

My competitor, once I got my project under way, was a neighbor, Johanna Ham, wife of Alexander Ham and mother of four children: Joey, Karen, Marvin, and Jimmy. Incurably optimistic, a compulsive prankster, and possessing a personal magnetism that attracted every creature to her, she was the type of person needed for every community's smooth functioning. When it became evident I would have to have someone to look in on my mother while I was at the office, I did not have far to go. Mrs. Ham lived right across the street, and she agreed to work in some visits to my place each day. I made my arrangements with her, never dreaming that in so doing I was opening my premises to a Fifth Column that would undermine the loyalty of every bird I possessed!

Like all clever undercover agents, she had infiltrated my ranks and was firmly entrenched before I realized what had taken place. The first inkling I had that mischief was afoot was when I noticed a change in the behavior of my first mynah bird, Snowball. I had purchased him some weeks previously and had been disappointed to see no immediate demonstration of the highly touted talking ability of his species. Not long after Mrs. Ham's visits began, however, he suddenly greeted me one evening with a rousing "Hi! How's my girl?" I was elated at this breakthrough until I realized that I had never said these words to him. Recalling that Frisky the parakeet had rejected me as a teacher, I was put immediately on the defensive. I was not long in discovering who was sabotaging my program. Mrs. Ham admitted these words were her standard greeting when she entered my front door, insisting, however, that they were addressed only to my mother and that she was as astonished as I that Snowball had picked them up. Soon other equally innocent phrases, such as "I'll see you in a little bit" and "I'll be right back, okay?" found their way into Snowball's vocabulary. Mrs. Ham's subversive activities were exposed increasingly to public scrutiny as Snowball enlarged his repertoire.

After my initial chagrin subsided I decided to make the best of a bad situation, and when I analyzed it closely, I found the situation was not really too bad. My bird was picking up a vocabulary, Mrs. Ham had learned the ABC's of mynah care, and I was freed from the confinement of staying home to provide lessons. With my mother or my friends I made a number of trips and took part in various social activities, which I probably would have passed up had I been "going steady" with Snowball.

When I got my second mynah, Audubon, however, I re-

My rival Mrs. Ham and Edgar the raven.

solved I would keep him out of Mrs. Ham's clutches. I had acquired Henry the crow at about the same time and was having difficulty adjusting to keeping so large a bird in the house. Thus, I more than welcomed any assistance Mrs. Ham could give me with him, and I felt that he would keep her so occupied she would have no time to alienate the affections of the new mynah. Nevertheless, I put Audubon in my bedroom where she would have little contact with him except when changing the papers in his cage and providing water and his ration of mynah meal. Then I urged her to enter a joint project with me: to get the crow to say his name, Henry. As it turned out, the crow never said a very satisfactory "Henry," but Miss America the magpie, from her listening post in the kitchen, did, and for some reason that word became her favorite expletive whenever she was upset or excited.

That fall I sprained my back carrying a bag of bird seed into my garage. To ease the pangs of muscle spasms that followed, I applied ice packs to my back and, to make the pack more comfortable to lie on, spent considerable time on the kitchen floor pounding big ice cubes into little ones. Any sort of activity that involved brandishing some kind of "weapon"—even a fly swatter—upset Miss America, and during my ice-pounding sessions with the hammer she would jump about in her cage exclaiming "Henry! Henry!" Mrs. Ham soon got into the act, finding she could evoke the same response from the magpie by dancing about in the kitchen tapping on the floor with a broom handle and saying "Henry, Henry, Henry."

This maneuver did not arouse my suspicions, but it turned out later to be a diversionary tactic employed to achieve another "coup." Audubon was beginning to utter some human sounds, and I hoped to be present on the occasion when he said his first word. Hearing him one morning commencing one of his "jam" sessions, I crept to the bedroom door in anticipation of the great event. What did I hear? "Henry, Henry, Henry," with every nuance of Mrs. Ham's inflection! Once again I was but an also-ran. It was then that I realized Mrs. Ham had something going for her that I lacked.

My ego had not recovered from that blow when Audubon threw me another curve that showed how low I really ranked on his totem pole. One week in the late fall Mrs. Ham said she had a cold and was staying away from the birds as much as possible to avoid spreading her germs to them. She did continue, however, to feed and water the various birds. Shortly thereafter I heard Audubon making a strange sound, but I did not recognize it until he gave the sound in her presence. "Why, that's my cough," she exclaimed. Since she had had the cough for only a week and had been in my bedroom only briefly each day during that interval, it was evident that Audubon had done a very quick "take" of the sound. I was glad to get this item on record, however, realizing that a coughing bird would make an interesting conversation piece during my bird programs.

It was not until later, when I developed a cough myself, that all the implications of Audubon's behavior became evident. I caught some type of virus infection and stayed at home coughing day and night for two months before going back to work. During this time Audubon also coughed periodically, but his cough was invariably patterned after Mrs. Ham's long-gone cough, not mine. There was no mistaking the two sounds: my cough was short and choppy; hers was loose and leisurely.

At first I was deeply chagrined at Audubon's indifference to my long-sustained efforts in contrast to his response to Mrs. Ham. However, that spring when I was again active, I was asked to present a bird program at a garden club, during which I dramatized my unsuccessful competition with Mrs. Ham. My audience chuckled at my statement that no one could imagine what it does to one's ego to realize that even his cough is judged inferior to another's. I knew then that I had something going for me after all; the very ludicrousness of my predicament made for a much better story than if I simply had a list of uneventful successes to relate.

My inferiority complex received a lift with the addition of Edgar the raven to my collection. Although "Hi" and "Hi-ya"—Mrs. Ham's stock greetings to the birds—soon appeared in his vocabulary, his chief items—"Nevermore, Edgar" and "You're a bad boy"—were unmistakably in my voice. He also had a display with which he frequently greeted me, spreading out his wings and vibrating his tail until it became a blur to the eye. In the wild this display probably is a recognition ritual, but I interpreted it, in Edgar's case, to be also a friendly gesture or sign of affection toward me. The correctness of my deduction was soon confirmed, as usual by an unfavorable comparison with Mrs. Ham. After one of her impromptu visits she remarked that she should say goodbye to her "kids" before leaving. I knew that Henry the crow was especially partial to her and had heard him greet her with a long, drawn-out "Wu-oooo" which he never accorded me. Hearing him give this sound when she went into his room, I walked to the door to observe his behavior. I was startled to see he was spreading his wings and waggling his tail in the exact display of Edgar, batting his eyes ecstatically as Mrs. Ham stroked his head. Until that moment I had not realized that the two related birds had this behavior in common. Mrs. Ham then mischievously suggested that I see if I could elicit the same reaction. Imitating her voice and manner as best I could, I slowly thrust my hand between the bars of Henry's cage, speaking soothingly the while, only to be rebuffed by a snapping beak and an angry caw. Miffed, I went back to my bedroom to enjoy the more satisfying company of Edgar, who at least thought enough of me to waggle his tail!

Even loyal Miss America the magpie fell under the spell of the charming temptress. In Miss A's third year, when I had supposed she had passed the learning period, she nearly doubled the vocabulary I had taught her by adding the phrases "Want some more to eat?" and "Just a minute," words spoken by Mrs. Ham as she prepared bird menus at the sink beside Miss America's cage.

Miss A's defection to my rival's camp did more than deflate my ego—it raised serious misgivings as to the validity of my research. What I was learning, of course, was the truth, but was it the whole truth? What might all of my birds have learned had they been living in the Ham household instead of my own? Any way I looked at it, my birds obviously were not living in an environment conducive to developing their full potential. Suddenly I felt sorry for myself. "All I lack to be totally unfitted for this job," I grumbled, "is an allergy to feathers!"

A humorous thought occurred to me in time to banish my

If Henry could have "talked" with this wild crow, Mrs. Ham would have easily had yet another "fan" club member.

mood of self-pity. The smaller of two national car rental concerns in the United States had attracted the public's attention to its own services by cleverly exploiting its secondary position. "When you're No. 2 in this business," the ads read, "you try harder." To fortify myself in the coming battle for my birds' affections, I prepared a big peanut butter and jelly sandwich, an item not ordinarily on my diet because of its high caloric content. As I savored its gooey goodness I mapped my future strategy. "I'll 'try harder!'" I said.

Mynahs can copy the human voice with great accuracy—often with unexpected results.

CHAPTER III

Nature's Tape Recorder De Luxe

In these days of easy access to tape decks and other types of recording equipment, almost anyone can listen to his own voice if he wishes. However, except for the ephemeral echo and until Thomas A. Edison spoke his immortal lines about Mary's little lamb onto a tinfoil cylinder, the only people who had ever heard a reproduction of their own voices were those in contact with the various species of talking birds. Of these comparatively few individuals, those living in southern Asia and adjacent islands, home of the greater Indian hill and Java mynahs, were the ones privileged to hear their own voices reproduced with the greatest fidelity.

The mynahs are not the best known nor earliest known talkers; so far as the western world is concerned, that distinction is held by the various parrots of Asia and Africa, whose fame was spread abroad by traders and conquerors. Mynahs were undoubtedly popular as pets in their native land, but the difficulty of feeding and transporting them resulted in their fame being confined for centuries to their homeland. The development of mynah pellets and mynah meal, coupled with faster means of transportation, started these birds on their mission of captivating pet owners in every clime by their astounding ability to reproduce the sound dearest to the heart of every human being—his own voice.

The mynah is not a beautiful bird nor does he project the adorable image of the budgie or cockatiel, but he does have his own distinctive features that hold up and become more attractive under prolonged exposure to his personality. When I decided I must have something around the house that talked besides myself, it was natural that I should consider the mynah family. This decision was influenced by the fact that I had just made the acquaintance of an energetic little woman, Anna Curtis, who, although in her mid-70's, was still operating her pet shop a few blocks from my home. Her reputation for having good birds had resulted in a thriving business, and she had expanded her trade to include special orders for exotic birds. Every spring, when the new crop of young greater Indian hill mynahs reached the shores of California, she ordered a dozen of these potential orators, and pandemonium reigned in her establishment with the arrival of the shipment, usually around Mother's Day.

As I became better acquainted with her, she allowed me the privilege of going back into her aviary to inspect the new arrivals. She had three or four climbing over each other in each cage, their wide-open mouths entreating any passer-by for a handout. For the first two weeks it was a full-time job hand-feeding them until they got the idea of picking up the dampened mynah meal by themselves. Eventually, Mrs. Curtis allowed me to take part in the feeding routine and after mastering my initial apprehension that my whole finger, along with the gob of mynah meal stuck on its tip, would disappear forever through the cavernous portals of the youngsters' deep orange beaks, I found the operation an exhilarating one. There were always several especially energetic individuals in each shipment, and during the almost continuous feeding operation it was no easy matter to keep them from bouncing out the cage doors or to round them up afterwards among the feed sacks, extra cages, and other supplies stored in the backroom of the average pet shop.

As a result of the insight thus gained regarding mynah

Neatness is not one of the mynah's claims to fame.

care and behavior, I acquired sufficient confidence to take the next logical step and purchased one of the fledglings, along with the special mynah cage best suited to the needs of these birds. In what I considered a clever bit of overstatement I named him "Snowball" and commenced my talking bird project in earnest.

As chronicled elsewhere, Snowball did not respond to my tutoring. Thanks, however, to the Ham clan, he did eventually acquire a vocabulary which I recorded as his contribution to the sound effects I proposed to include with the results of my studies.

Since mynahs, because of their diet, are rather messy birds to have around the house and take up considerable space, I intended to conclude this part of my investigations with observations based on my experience with Snowball only. However, about three summers later, when I went into Mrs. Curtis's shop to inspect the new mynah fledglings, she pointed to a dejected individual huddled alone in a corner of a cage and gloomily stated he had apparently been injured during shipment since his left wing was paralyzed. My sympathies were aroused by the forlorn little cripple and, reasoning that his useless wing could not have any effect on his talking potential, I decided to give the mynahs another fling. I purchased a second cage and brought him home. To compensate for his insignificant appearance I named him after the great American naturalist, Audubon, and set up his headquarters in my bedroom. Here he spent his first summer and, like Snowball, gave scant attention to my efforts to educate him.

My bird elocution program took a recess that winter when I developed pneumonia and spent three months at home or in the hospital. To avoid exposing Audubon to my germs, I moved him into my guest bedroom where, with the eternal indifference of Nature to the personal problems of mankind, he continued to develop his inner resources at his own pace and without any assistance from me.

During my enforced bed rest and recuperation I was in an excellent position to be aware of Audubon's accomplishments, and I soon noticed he was giving a long series of unintelligible imitations of some conversation whose origin was a mystery to me. One day Jimmy Ham came over to borrow the tinsnips. As he dived out the door he rattled off some explanation of his purpose, and I suddenly realized that his was the voice that Audubon was imitating. But where was Jimmy, and what was he doing that gave Audubon an opportunity to hear him? I set up my microphone in Audubon's room, turned on the recorder, and took down a long series of his observations. I then summoned the Ham family to listen to the results. With their firsthand knowledge of the family's routine, activities, and points of disagreement they were able to translate many of Audubon's comments, with the result that we soon had a very red-faced little boy on our hands.

I knew Mrs. Ham and Joey divided the responsibilities of

caring for my birds, Mrs. Ham doing the indoor work and her son Joey taking over for the birds outside. What I did not know was that Jimmy, already a budding businessman, had volunteered to help Joey take care of the outside birds and share in the profits. Being the smaller of the brothers, however, he had concluded he was doing more than his share of work, and he did not intend to suffer in silence. Audubon, now stationed in a bedroom with French doors opening onto the backyard, was in a position to overhear every word. "There's nothing wrong with you at all, Joe, do it yourself," Audubon intoned with every inflection of Jimmy's complaining voice. "You don't have to go to school yet"—this comment developed from the fact that Jimmy's grade school opened earlier than Joey's high school. Now and then there was a remark in a deeper voice, "Why don't you go home?" indicating that the patience of even the long-suffering Joey could wear thin. "All right, Karen will drop us off!" Karen pounced on this apparently innocent prediction since she knew what prompted it. Al-

though Jimmy's school was located within walking distance, the young man much preferred to be chauffeured to its doors and spent considerable time wheedling his brother or sister into driving him to school.

"So you think I'm an easy mark, do you?" Karen said accusingly. Jimmy ducked his head into a pillow, then announced he was going home. Curiosity as to what else might be on the tape, however, impelled him to stay to the bitter end.

Fortunately, the sharp-eared tape recorder next revealed that Jimmy did indeed carry on part of his work without complaining. "The doves need water, Joe, I'll get it." "I've shut the garage door." Then a very significant statement, since Jimmy probably said it but once: "Open the door, Joe"—a pause, then—"I think that Joe is deaf!" Jimmy recalled making this statement. With a dish in each hand he had approached the back door of the garage where Joey was feeding the crow and magpie, and he called to Joey to open the door. Since Joey apparently did not hear him, Jimmy had added the comment to himself, "I think that Joe is deaf." There were a number of other remarks on the tape that were not clear enough for the Hams to identify, but they obviously were observations that Jimmy had made in the run-together sentences that young people often use in communicating with one another, clear to themselves and presumably to Audubon but not intelligible to behind-the-times oldsters.

This interlude in Audubon's development was a source of entertainment in an otherwise long and humdrum winter, and it also required me to reassess my conclusions about a bird's learning processes. It is generally agreed that repetition plays an important part in teaching a bird to talk, yet Audubon had picked up casual remarks that were certainly not repeated in precisely the same terms each time they were made, although the boys may have wrangled over the same subjects at different times. While Jimmy may have said more than once "Open the door, Joe," he certainly did not repeat "I think that Joe is deaf."

It is also evident that the impression made on a bird's brain of a spoken phrase and its subsequent retention are different from those governing man's conscious recollection of a phrase. I knew that had I overheard a conversation in a foreign tongue, the only way I could have retained any portion of the meaningless sounds would have been to repeat them phonetically as soon as I heard them. Even then, in all probability, once I ceased to concentrate on the sounds I could never have repeated them again unless, like some Lost Chord, they surfaced later from my subconscious mind. In contrast, once sounds were programmed into Audubon's brain, he apparently could do a "print-out" any time he chose, and he continued to repeat many of the phrases, especially the "garage door" part, for years afterward.

This capacity of a mynah to do the unexpected accounts for the fascination he holds for the human race. Unlike many of the parrots, he does not continue to pick up new sounds throughout his lifetime. Unfortunately, too, as he grows older he tends to drop some of his vocabulary. But that first wonderful year or two, when his owner can follow his progress from his first efforts—spoken in a strikingly "baby" voice—to his later sophisticated offerings uttered with all the authority of an adult, and speculate on what the brain behind those inscrutable eyes will bring forth next, makes the ownership of a mynah worthwhile and will always assure for him a spot in the human family that no other pet can fill.

The European starling is an active, hardy, and highly intelligent bird, but can it talk?

CHAPTER IV
Two-Timed by Mortimer

"I'll have a starling shall be taught to speak nothing but 'Mortimer.'" By inserting these words in his play *Henry IV*, written in the late 1590's, Shakespeare unwittingly launched, some three hundred years later, a band of unwilling feathered pilgrims to the New World. Seventy years after that, the same words launched me on a sometimes frustrating but always fascinating endeavor to put those words into action.

The background of this remark, which takes place early in the first act of Shakespeare's play, is as follows: Mortimer, Earl of March and brother-in-law of Lord Percy, also known as Hotspur, has been captured during an uprising of the Welsh and is being held for ransom, set at no less than the release by the King of all Welsh prisoners. Evidently, Mortimer is rather low on the political and social totem pole, since the King does not consider him worth the price and refuses to bargain with the rebels. Hotspur is either on unusually good terms with his brother-in-law or else is being urged by his sister to use his influence with the King to obtain the release of her husband. At any rate, Hotspur intervenes on Mortimer's behalf but is given the royal brush-off. In a tantrum Hotspur relates to his companions the King's rebuff. "He said he would not ransom Mortimer," Hotspur rails; "Forbade my tongue to speak of Mortimer. But I will find him when he lies asleep and in his ear I'll holloa 'Mortimer!' Nay, better yet, I'll have a starling shall be taught to speak nothing but 'Mortimer' and give it him, to keep his anger still in motion."

These lines—the only reference Shakespeare ever made

"Nay, better yet, I'll have a starling shall be taught to speak nothing but 'Mortimer' and give it him, to keep his anger still in motion."

to the starling—did not escape the attention of a Shakespearean enthusiast in the 1890's who decided to honor the Bard by importing into the United States every bird mentioned in his writings. Skylarks, nightingales, thrushes, and others also made their unsought-for entry into this country, only to vanish into oblivion soon after their release—all but the starling, which adapted with its accustomed flexibility to the new environment and began its inexorable infiltration into every habitable portion of the land.

In all fairness to the Shakespearean admirer it should be stated that his were not the only starlings introduced into this country during the decade of the 1890's. However, the importation sparked by Shakespeare was the most romantic, and when I began my love affair with the talking birds, the tale of Hotspur and his proposed revenge caught my imagination. Visions of a young lad playing with a starling in a thatch-roofed cottage in Elizabethan England went through my mind—far different times and a different world than mine; only the bird had not changed. Shakespeare's starlings looked and acted the same as those at my bird feeder each morning.

"If Shakespeare could train a starling, I can too," I exclaimed impetuously to an engineer with whom I was discussing my plans. My listener, a patron of the arts as well as the sciences, raised his eyebrows. "Are you inferring you can do anything Shakespeare could do?" he inquired.

That, I assured him, most certainly was not what I meant. But there was another angle from which I could approach this challenge. In the vast display of homage paid to Shakespeare, surely there was some niche wherein I could make a contribution. Nobody, to the best of my knowledge, had ever attempted to teach a starling to say "Mortimer." Here was my opportunity to further my own project and at the same time add to the accumulation of data on natural history as depicted by Shakespeare. I might even report my findings to the Royal Society for the Study of Shakespearean Natural History, if any such organization existed. In the grip of this inspiration I gave free rein to my imagination and plunged into a world peopled with knights and knaves, heroes and cravens, kings and commoners—in short, as I understood it, the world of Shakespeare.

The circumstances surrounding my first candidate smoldered with all the elements of medieval intrigue, dastardly deeds, and murder most foul in a manner not envisaged even by Shakespeare—infanticide by a deadly potion unknowingly administered by the parents. I received a call to pick up a baby starling which had just been rescued from a puddle. Sensing the beginnings of my new project, I responded enthusiastically and was soon in possession of a fledgling starling. However, I soon realized that my hoped-for Mortimer had already been "done in," probably by a diet of insects which contained lethal concentrations of pesticides. He weakened rapidly despite my solicitude and soon quit this life so fraught with perils for both bird and man.

My second prospect was a freedom-loving individual, wise beyond his years, who took the advice of Lady Macbeth and stayed not on the method of his going. I was called by a friend who had given a young starling free run of her apartment, where she conducted a home decorating business. Her customers, she found, expressed a certain reluctance to purchase materials over which a starling had scampered, and she had decided to place her pet elsewhere. When I arrived at her house, however, I found her wandering about in her backyard, obviously searching for something. She informed me that she had taken the bird outdoors while she worked in her garden. On previous occasions he had stayed inside the fence, returning to her on command. Now, however, he had failed to respond, and she feared he had taken leave without any formal farewell. Such proved to be the case and I returned home empty-handed.

Here, a starling
makes like a
hummingbird—

...as he snatches a
mealworm in flight.

The Shakespearean character portrayed by my next candidate was hard to establish. I had put on a program for a garden club, during which I described my talking bird study and my search for a prospective Mortimer starling. The next day one of the members who had been present at the meeting called to tell me that William Shakespeare had been rescued from a cat that morning and was now in a box under the kitchen table awaiting my arrival. I hastened to her address, lifted the bird out of his cardboard prison, and, since he seemed rather lethargic, gave him first-aid by pushing some dogfood into his beak. He swallowed this offering with scornful indifference, and his whole attitude projected a royal aloofness that spurns combat with an inferior personage. "Haughty and disdainful" was the description given by a disgruntled acquaintance of a medieval princess who later became a famous queen. Shakespeare had written of kings and queens and people of high estate. "Clearly born to the purple royal," I said of this third and healthy prospect, whom I straightway christened "Mortimer" and whom I set up in a cage in my living room, within hearing distance of his cousin Snowball.

But Shakespeare also wrote of knaves and rascals and ordinary human beings, and it became evident that this young Mortimer was made of very ordinary stuff. Clearly he lived more for his stomach than for his soul. Anyone who has witnessed evidences of a starling's appetite is bound to say in disbelief, "He's got to be kidding; no bird that small could eat so much and still be hungry." His diet consisted of canned dogfood, hard-boiled egg, and grapes, and he would "attack" rather than simply eat the mixture, using a caliper-like opening and closing of his beak that scattered the contents of his dish both inside and out of the cage. In this respect he became my most messy tenant. His efforts at personal cleanliness, unfortunately, also made this designation appropriate. No one can truthfully refer to a starling as a "dirty bird." If frequency of bathing means

Mortimer Starling cannot control his excitement as he waits for me to add the "frosting"—hard-boiled egg—to his menu.

anything, a starling is almost sterilizingly clean. In addition to splashing the water out of his bathing dish, he would quite literally "plow up" the soggy paper on the bottom of his cage, again using his beak as calipers. If any water remained in the dish after his ablutions, Mortimer soon sloshed the rest of it out by prying under the dish with his beak, the strength of his jaws being sufficient to permit him to "hitch" the dish along for several inches before he ceased his instinctive probing for food.

But the dream of getting an emphatic "Mortimer" on my tape enabled me to overlook the inconvenience caused by his personal idiosyncracies. I began his elocution lessons immediately, playing a tape recording of the word "Mortimer," saying the word to him personally as often as possi-

This long-tailed glossy starling would also probably not be an outstanding "student of voice."

ble, and enlisting the aid of Mrs. Ham in my campaign. But in spite of the many times he heard this word, his first "human" utterance was "Henry." Both Mrs. Ham and I were saying "Henry" endlessly to the young crow, in hopes he would learn to say at least the first part of his name, "Henry Ward Beecher." Audubon the mynah bird was at the height of his learning ability and picked up the word, and Miss America, in the kitchen, carried on the round robin by making "Henry" her favorite exclamation.

Bombarded on all sides by either "Henry" or "Mortimer," with typical contrariness the starling chose the less important of the two words, and I began to get the impression, at unexpected intervals, that I was hearing a mini-voiced "Henry" coming from his corner. However, proof that he was actually saying it was as difficult to obtain as a photograph of a flying saucer, since the tape recorder was never in operation at the time I thought I heard it.

Rewards for the person working with birds of only marginal talking ability come few and far between. I felt I fully deserved the gift Mortimer gave me on his first Christmas. Enjoying the luxury of sleeping late, I was roused by a series of "Henry, Henry's" coming from the front room and too "small" to be made by the magpie. I set up my recording equipment, and before the morning was over I had tangible proof that Mortimer indeed was saying "Henry." It was fortunate for my project that Reverend Beecher's first name was Henry and that I had decided to name the crow after him, since the word fitted in very appropriately with my Mortimer-King Henry bit.

But I still had no "Mortimer" for my record. The rest of the winter I continued to "saturate" the starling with the word "Mortimer." Mrs. Ham joined my campaign, and Audubon, ever alert to her voice, was soon saying "Mortimer." Again Miss America picked up an oft-repeated word and gave a very creditable version of it. Once more a word had "caught on," but this time the starling was not impressed. It was not until spring that Mrs. Ham confirmed my suspicion that Mortimer was finally saying the all-important word. We both agreed, however, that it was in an incredibly small voice.

On Easter morning I again set up my recording equipment in anticipation of another present from Mortimer. But Mortimer had other items on his agenda that carried a higher priority than merely being the first of his kind to enact a scene by the world's greatest playwright. For one thing, I had just changed the paper in his cage and put in fresh water, and this called for a bath and subsequent "plowing" of the terrain. But in spite of these diversions and much "time out" to inspect the menu and look for grapes, he uttered enough "Mortimer's" on the tape to prove that he was saying the word. He continued to say it at intervals, sometimes when the recorder was running, but even with the volume turned up until the power roar reached an undesirable level, the word was barely audible on the

Hotspur had no idea of how difficult it is to teach a starling to talk.

46

tape. No one would expect so small a bird to have as strong a voice as, say, a magpie, but it was most frustrating to hear the ridiculous squeak with which he said "Mortimer," followed by a "Henry," "come back," or "I'll be right back" in a voice loud enough for anyone with normal hearing to understand.

I fretted over this exasperating quirk of nature until one day I "got the picture," and the character this bird was supposed to represent came into focus. After all, Shakespeare had written this script, not I. This silly little starling wasn't cast in the hero's role; no feats of valor, no storming of the gates to glory for him. Rather, the role of that blustering, fun-loving, gluttonous, amorous reveler, Sir John Falstaff, was the one in which Mortimer the starling was most at home. That wily opportunist Falstaff would never have risked the King's displeasure by irritating him with the name of an inferior whom he wished to dismiss from his mind. On the other hand, almost everyone realizes that the sweetest word any person can hear is his own name. What better way to win a king's favor than by regaling him with repetitions of his name?

But what about Mortimer Starling's obligation to me—the one who had organized, sponsored, and financed this whole production and had elevated him above millions of his compatriots on the assumption that he would reward me with an acceptable rendition of the word "Mortimer"? Well, hadn't he kept faith with me by saying the word, regardless of whether it was audible to everyone or not? After all, I *had* failed to specify, even in the small print, how many decibels must be attained.

My report, had I been making one, to the Royal Society for the Study of Shakespearean Natural History, would have been short and to the point: If you're thinking of bugging someone by teaching a starling to say "Mortimer"—forget it!

"What-cha doin'?"

CHAPTER V

Hello, Picklepuss

I fell in love with the rose-breasted cockatoo or "galah" of Australia when I saw one in a petting zoo playing a weekend stand at a neighboring shopping center. He was clinging to one side of his cage, enviously watching the spectators clustered around his more colorful relatives, the macaws. When he saw he had acquired an audience of his own, he hitched his way to my side of the cage and appealingly thrust out his foot to "shake hands." I knew then that I would never be satisfied until I, too, owned such a bird.

At the same time, however, I realized that my wish almost certainly would be unfulfilled. For years the importation of any parrot-type birds into the United States had been restricted severely. On the other side of the Pacific, Australia had recently put into effect a ban on the exportation of any of its native birds. A friend of mine, smitten with a young sulphur-crested cockatoo in a pet shop but unable to meet its $700 tab, had appealed to a friend in Australia to send her one direct from its homeland. His reply, while humorous, was short and to the point: "Ask me to do anything for you except send you one of our parrots," he wrote. "It would cost me my job, my family, my life!" My own investigations into the subject indicated prohibitive prices for the few cockatoos of any species raised by local breeders in the United States. So I gloomily concluded that for me a rose-breasted cockatoo would remain my Vision Fugitive, my Impossible Dream.

Into this setting of inflexible regulations and against the gathering clouds of the Newcastle Disease quarantine, my bird suddenly flashed on silver wings. I met a biology professor who, several years previously, had completed a tour as exchange teacher in Australia. During his assignment he had acquired two pairs of rose-breasted cockatoos and two pairs of rosellas. The length of his sojourn entitled him to declare the birds as personal property which could be removed legally from the country on completion of his tour of duty. Even so, it was only after endless red tape on both sides of the Pacific that he finally got his eight birds onto American soil. One of the female rose-breasts met with an accident, leaving the professor with two males and one female. He naturally had entertained hopes of breeding the birds but now found himself confronted with an avian triangle. One of the males showed much interest in the remaining female, but she spurned his attention and cast, instead, a coy eye towards the second male. However, this male was no Don Juan in feathers, and he scorned the advances of the brazen female, preferring to join the first male in a wood-carving contest. Frustrated, the professor began to entertain the idea that if the second male were not around, the female might be more responsive to the attentions of the first male. Upon learning this, I informed the professor that I was much interested in the extra male and would like to be given first choice should he decide to sell the bird. Understandably, the professor hesitated before parting with such an irreplaceable asset. For two years my bird fluttered tantalizingly just out of reach—a pink cloud on the horizon. Finally, his owner accepted an assignment in another state, informed me that he would sell the bird, and named a price I could meet. I did not quibble for a moment; the fact that, against such odds, so rare a bird should come within my range seemed to be a good omen for the success of my project. I set out on the fifty-mile drive to the professor's home town, accompanied by Mrs. Ham, whose charisma, I felt, would smooth the transition to the bird's new quarters. On the way up we pondered what to name him, but found, upon our arrival, that he had already learn-

This profile of a rose-breasted cockatoo shows off the bird's small features and flower-like crest.

ed his name, Picklepuss. With the slightest encouragement he would exclaim, in a very clear voice, "Hello Picklepuss, what'cha doin'? come on, dance, goodbye," and go into the rhythmic "two-step" that is a normal maneuver with many of the larger parrots. Rose-breasted cockatoos are not considered to be good talkers, yet Picklepuss had acquired quite an adequate repertoire, exclusively, the family told me, from the grandmother, who had been a frequent visitor in their home when they lived in another state.

On the drive back, Picklepuss chattered away in the back seat of the car and, upon arrival at his new address, behaved in the manner characteristic of inhabitants of the Old West or perhaps the equally informal citizens of the Outback of Australia; it was evident that home was anywhere his cage was, and he never met a stranger. I had resolved that for the first few days I would not take him out of his cage, but he insisted on walking down my arm and out the cage door and soon was perching on my shoulder whispering "what-cha doin'?" I feared he had caught cold in the car on the way home and was too hoarse to speak aloud; my fears were allayed when I discovered that, like human beings, he could "whisper" as well as "shout." I also found that the heavy feathering around his flanks held an abundance of a powder-like substance which covered my fingers as though I had thrust them into a box of face powder. This substance—a breakdown of some secondary feathering—is a distinguishing feature of cockatoo plumage and accounts for the delicately frosted appearance unique to cockatoos.

It would be hard to find another bird that has a more attractive color combination than the rose-breasted cockatoo. Some other parrots have a greater variety of colors and present a more brilliant effect, but the rose-breast has points in his favor which enable him to more than hold his own in any parrot beauty contest. For one thing, he has finer features than many of the other cockatoos, in that his beak is rather small and delicately proportioned—for a parrot—resulting in a more "photogenic profile" than many of his larger relatives. And while the rose-breast's crest is not so conspicuous and highly colored as that of the Major Mitchell or the Moluccan cockatoo, when he flares it the delicate pink shadings and curly feathers composing it give the effect of looking into the heart of a full-blown pink peony.

Yes, Picklepuss had charms in abundance, and his friendliness and willingness to be handled gave him a high rating as a pet. As is the case with humans and animals alike, however, longer acquaintance did reveal some facets of his nature not immediately discernible on first meeting. I presently found that the childhood jingle about the little girl with the curl applied to galahs as well, only I rephrased it to read:

> There was a cockatoo and he had a little crest
> Right in the middle of his forehead.
> When he was good he was very, very good,
> And when he was bad he was horrid.

Private Eye Picklepuss works at enlarging his "peep space."

Picklepuss's behavior toward me when Mrs. Ham, my ever-present rival, was around gave me the first inkling of his split personality. He always went to her readily, of course, and one day I noticed him regarding me from her shoulder, with flared crest and what could only be termed a "baleful" eye. Suddenly, he flew at my head, tangled in my hair briefly, and returned to her shoulder. At first I thought he was trying to make the transition from her shoulder to my head, but when he repeated the performance a few minutes later there was no mistaking that his flailing wings and jabs into my hair with his beak signified an attack. I had read of these "cockatoo charges" and when Picklepuss one day flew clear across the room to nip me on the neck, I could understand why sturdy zoo keepers cringe before such an onslaught. I later found that his attacks were not leveled exclusively against me and that they could be triggered by a number of actions or nonactions. He apparently did not like to be ignored, and sometimes when I was preoccupied with other matters it appeared he launched an attack merely to provide a little excitement or to attract my attention. He also developed a fixation about hair and even bullied Mrs. Ham when she showed up with a new hair style. As for me, he apparently decided that my braids should be wound around my head, and if I attempted to "make" like an Indian in his presence, he soon reminded me of my status as a "Paleface." Although an up-to-date pet in most respects, he failed to rally to the banner that liberates men from the tyranny of the razor and the barber's shears, and I learned to keep him under close surveillance when showing my aviary to the unshorn and the unshaven.

The rosy-colored little tyrant was equally vigilant in defending his territory against interlopers. Some neighbors gave me their female canary-winged parakeet whose loud screeches got on their nerves. The little parrot was much interested in the Australian grass parakeets which I also housed in my basement, and she would liked to have spent all day frisking on top of their cage. Picklepuss decided this brassy little newcomer must be kept in her place, and

J.C. RIGLI
12-8-77

54

whenever he was out of his cage the resulting aerial chase gave much the effect of a bomber chasing a pursuit plane. Picklepuss was no slouch at flying, but the smaller size and speed of the canary-wing gave her greater maneuverability. The chase invariably ended with the canary-wing, panting but unscathed, peering from behind some perch, while Picklepuss strutted victoriously on top of the parakeet cage, a dog-in-the-manger gesture since Picklepuss otherwise took no notice of his countrymen. However, recognizing the possibility of either bird knocking itself out, or worse, in these high-speed maneuvers, I decided to stagger their hours of liberty. Since the canary-wing did not go exploring in the room but stayed close to the parakeets, I did not cage her even when I was not in the room. However, I could not extend this privilege to Picklepuss. He was prone to go prowling on the floor, where I feared he might pick up some unnoticed piece of debris which could be hazardous to his health. On the other hand, at the higher elevations of the room, where he was safer, his activities were hazardous to the furniture. I had a carpenter make frames for two of my bird displays; in a few seconds' time, when I was briefly distracted, Picklepuss neatly ripped off a long splinter from each. The door I gave him a free hand with, since I had another the same size in my garage which I could use as a replacement, if necessary. However, the enthusiasm with which Picklepuss set about paring that door down to size made me wonder whether I should not have more than one spare door on hand. Digging the sharp tip of his upper mandible into the wood for an anchor, Picklepuss then used his lower mandible as a plane, ripping splinters as much as a foot long off the top of the door, the space beneath often taking on the appearance of the floor in a planing mill.

This propensity for ripping up even tough materials makes the larger parrots among the most difficult to house, requiring heavy metallic structures to minimize such dam-

Picklepuss pouts when Greenjeans insists on getting into his "come-on-dance" routine.

Picklepuss takes time out to inspect the fruits of his labors.

age. Galahs also have other destructive habits which work to their disadvantage when conducted in the croplands of Australia. A band of these birds moving through a field of grain or other cockatoo delicacies can soon riddle the crop, with the result that they are not popular with the farmers of that continent and often carry a bounty on their heads.

However, as a pet the galah still calls forth admiration and delight among those people fortunate enough to own one. The late King George V of England was so enchanted by a pet galah that he kept it in his company as much as royal protocol would permit. As the lucky owner of one of these lovely birds, I can appreciate the enthusiasm of the King for his pet and I am sure he would have been fully in agreement with the opinion that the rose-breasted cockatoo is indeed worthy to walk and talk with kings.

A cockatiel is indeed one of the most pleasant and enjoyable birds to have as a pet.

CHAPTER VI

The Pied Piper of Birdland

Of the cockatiel it may be said, to paraphrase William Jennings Bryan's famous tribute to the strawberry, "Doubtless God could have made a cuter bird, but doubtless God never did." With his expression of perpetual alertness and his photogenic profile, enhanced by his brightly "rouged" cheek patches and plumed crest, Australia's cockatiel or quarrion reminds me of a brightly painted, wound-up toy soldier.

Since a cockatiel is not a loner and must have either abundant human attention or companionship of his own kind to be content, I did not intend to work with a cockatiel until I had retired. However, three years short of my projected retirement date, the very bird I envisioned dropped into my lap. One of Mrs. Curtis's customers reported that his pair of cockatiels had produced two young, one a normal, gray bird that was out on its own and the other a half-feathered, white runt that was still in the nest box. Fearing the parents would desert the retarded youngster, the customer asked Mrs. Curtis to come out and appraise the situation. Much intrigued by this development, I volunteered to drive her to his house the following evening. We found the white nestling, naked as a jaybird except for the long flight and tail feathers, crouching in the nest box and hissing vehemently when we removed him for examination. Mrs. Curtis agreed that in all probability he would henceforth have to be hand-fed, and I saw all eyes turning toward me as his appointed guardian. It was, I knew, a golden opportunity, but why, I wondered, did opportunity always knock too early or too late for me? Nevertheless, I took the bird home, soaked some nestling food in warm water, and administered his first artificial feeding. He showed no enthusiasm for this operation, and I foresaw a repetition of a scene I had enacted many times: bending every effort to keep a valued bird alive, only to watch it steadily weaken and die.

By the end of the week, in spite of Mrs. Ham's ministrations in the daytime, the cycle I had predicted for the bird was nearing completion. Although at times he ate reasonably well, he obviously was not getting enough nourishment, and when I grasped his wing-tips I found they were cold and clammy, a sure sign of ebbing vitality. In desperation I abandoned the nestling food and mixed up a helping of the baby cereal that I fed to young doves. To my jubilation he ate this mixture heartily.

I soon discovered, however, that the youngster was as erratic in his acceptance of the baby food as he was of the nestling food, and I realized that something must be lacking in my nursery routine. Out of a traumatic year's exposure to the only course in higher mathematics I ever attempted—algebra—all I can recall is that certain equations contain an unknown factor X, and by prescribed manipulations of the other elements in the equation, the mysterious "Lady X" can be persuaded to reveal her identity. Applying this hazy recollection to my current predicament, I realized that there must be an unknown X quantity in my feeding formula which I must solve if my bird was to survive. When one day he accepted a straight mixture of the baby food and then at the next feeding disassociated himself from precisely the same mixture, I felt I had narrowed down the constituents in the case to where I should be able to pin down the offending element. I could think of nothing that varied between the two feedings except perhaps temperature. I poured some more warm water into the mixture and offered it to him again at a temperature considerably warmer than I ordinarily used in my feeding operations. He

60

Streaky's "passport" photo.

gulped it down, underscoring his satisfaction with a series of low chuckles, evidently the cockatiel equivalent of "yum-yum." The riddle was solved: no lukewarm "soup" or "coffee" for him. Future feedings were routine so long as the temperature of the food was to his liking; if not, he would cease his chuckling and guzzling right in mid-feeding and turn his back on the whole performance.

Once his survival was assured, finding a suitable name for him was the first order of business, and Mrs. Ham soon provided a satisfactory moniker. Located as we are near the campus of a large university, we were well aware of the highly scholastic and erudite activity known as "streaking," an activity popular that year among some college students. In fact, the community had been promised a demonstration on a recent Sunday morning, which did not

61

take place as scheduled because Mother Nature, apparently to test the devotion of her disciples, sent a snowstorm which resulted in cancellation of the event. Mrs. Ham stated that our little white bird basically met the chief requirement of the sect—nudity—and christened him "Streaky." For over a month I feared his nakedness was going to be permanent; then a hint of orange feathering appeared around his ears, suggesting better times ahead. Wishing to document his transition from bare skin to complete feathering, I took him along when I went to a photography studio to have my first passport picture taken. "I'd like to have you snap him at his worst, so I will have a comparison later on," I told the photographer. He took a second glance at his subject. "That," he stated pessimistically, "won't be hard to do." But even little Streaky had his pride, and when he was posed under the photographer's lights he refused to reveal his worst feature—a totally featherless neck, which, when extended, made him look like a small, white vulture. Consequently, the resulting photo came out only slightly less complimentary to its subject than are most ID pictures and could have been used for a cockatiel passport had such a document been required under bird import regulations.

It never occurred to me that I might have misclassified Streaky as to sex until, at age eleven months, "he" laid the first of a series of fourteen eggs. Thereafter Streaky exercised the prerogative conferred upon her by virtue of her true sex and laid numerous clutches of eggs. Her egg production declined after her third year, and Streaky was able to devote more of her attention to what was for me the more rewarding exercise of being the lovable pet for which a cockatiel is famous.

Since the whistling and talking ability of cockatiels has already been well documented, I decided not to explore the subject further. However, on one of my visits to Mrs. Curtis's shop she complained that among her latest shipment of cockatiels was a male with a slightly deformed lower mandible. Her supplier offered to take the bird back, but she feared that, since it obviously could not be used for breeding, the owner would destroy it. I shared her apprehensions. Since I had a spare cage at home, I took this second cockie and placed him in the basement, which I called my "Australian Wing" since it housed Picklepuss, Streaky, and a number of Australian grass parakeets. With Streaky in full view and so much other avian companionship available, I did not expect the new cockatiel to take any interest in people. On the contrary, however, he soon began to show a lively curiosity about me, coming to my side of the cage whenever I was near him. Apparently, with a social structure to his liking, he was free to notice any other interesting features in his environment.

One day when I was whistling the first bars of "Let's All Sing Like the Birdies Sing" to Sugarplum, a parakeet with a flair for imitation, I was startled to hear a creditable imitation of the tune coming from the opposite side of the room and realized that Cockie had joined my music class. A cockatiel's imitation of tunes is usually described as whistling, but to me it sounded more like piping—the legendary Pipes of Pan, no less. I could not imagine a more adorable pixie piping in a woodland glen and immediately christened my cockatiel "Peter Pan." The name was appropriate also because a distinct "peter-peter" is a feature of the cockatiel's natural repertoire.

I whistled at every opportunity all the sections of the chorus of "Let's All Sing Like the Birdies Sing," and Peter responded enthusiastically. When I came to "give yourself a treat" with its descending scale—the opposite of the pattern of the "tweet, tweet-tweet"—Peter threw up his wings and pattered around in his cage in a maneuver that was amusingly suggestive of a person frustrated with the dilemma: "Just when I learned all the answers, somebody changed all the questions." Eventually, I had all sections of the

63

"Let's all sing like the birdies sing!"—the Pied Piper himself doing his thing.

tune on tape at different spots and I set about assembling a version of the complete song. It was then I learned the difference between teaching speech and teaching music. Words are usually spoken in one key, the natural placement of the teacher's voice. Music, on the other hand, can be produced in various keys, and since I do not have absolute pitch, my lessons had varied in key, faithfully reproduced by Peter Pan. I found some very weird effects can be produced when sections of the same tune are assembled in different keys. It was "back to the drawing board" for Peter's music lessons, and I purchased a pitch pipe at a local music store to be sure I did not make the same mistake again. The reaction of the clerk to my comment that I would use the pitch pipe for teaching music to a bird was almost worth the price of the pipe.

After I had an acceptable "Let's All Sing Like the Birdies Sing" on tape, I decided to enlarge Peter's repertoire to cover everything from country music to grand opera. But Peter had other ideas. He had "a song" in his heart and, like that of Snow White's prince, it was "but one song." He persisted in whistling "Let's All Sing" long after I had

64

One of the most popular pets of the parrot family is the cockatiel; this is a normal gray cockatiel male.

abandoned it and was whistling "Happy Birthday To You." Finally acknowledging that I did not have a winner in that tune, I changed to another titled—depending on one's philosophy—"How Dry I Am" or "Oh Happy Day." Peter occasionally incorporated a few notes into his "birdies" piece, but he never whistled any recognizable part of the whole theme. At this point I became guilty of some anthropomorphizing: parakeets and cockatiels need to be reminded of their repertoire periodically by their owners; otherwise they begin to produce garbled versions. I felt sorry for Peter valiantly trying to keep alive "his song" with no cooperation from me. Worst of all, however, I noted that his joyous whistling sessions were becoming fewer and shorter. Fearing that he might abandon his whistling altogether, I burst forth in the old familiar refrain, and Peter soon followed suit with all his former exuberance. He had been nearly eleven months old when I commenced his music lessons and may have reached his learning peak.

Even though my plans for Peter's musical education did not materialize, such was the charm of his personality that I could not say I was disappointed by his performance. When he greeted me one morning with a husky "Hello baby," I knew that he could do no wrong. Other terms of endearment, such as "ya' little darling" and "hello darling" followed. I suspect that exclamations of affection are the most frequent items in a cockatiel's repertoire, for I doubt that even a strong man can avoid using some term of endearment—however salty—in referring to his pet cockatiel. The owners of one of the largest exotic bird farms in the United States wrote that if they had to give up every bird in their vast collection save one, they would unhesitatingly choose to keep a cockatiel. Most owners of cockatiels would agree with their choice. Certainly one of the most pleasant ways to relax from the pressures and realities of everyday life is to sit back and be charmed by the antics and the music of the "Pied Piper of Birdland."

66

CHAPTER VII
She Didn't Say

Through my good fortune in owning the previously mentioned Frosty, I am well aware of the amazing versatility of the male budgerigar as a talker, but I have not included a separate chapter on male budgies in this book. There are available already many publications on training budgerigars to talk, the assumption being that it is the males that will receive such attention since the females are usually dismissed as possessing little talking potential. In general, this latter conclusion is true; nevertheless, there are many instances of female budgies that talked very well. Knowing that the females which do talk have not received nearly as much publicity as their "chauvinist" mates and mindful of the trend towards equal status for women, I resolved that I would devote a chapter to the female budgie before finalizing my talking bird study. However, I had heard and read enough about the unpredictability of these little charmers to put them at the end of my list, until I had retired from my job and could launch an all-out effort in their direction. Before reaching that point, however, I had several opportunities to prove the correctness of my assumption that teaching a female budgie to talk would be a full-time job.

Over a period of about a year I had a whole "spate" of female budgies brought to my door. The first was a very lean and hungry yellow lutino, but both the date on her leg band, which indicated she was several years old, and her high-strung disposition made it evident that she was no candidate for my classes.

The next female that came into my possession was a wretched little amputee, which an acquaintance had noted

Wild budgerigars are green, but many other color variations have been developed; this is a young normal light blue budgie.

The budgerigar, *Melopsittacus undulatus,* has been known by many names, including budgie, Australian lovebird, and Australian shell parakeet; this is an adult normal light green male budgie.

huddling in a pool of blood in a cage at the pet department of a local store. She had evidently caught her leg band on a projection in the cage, and in her struggles to free herself had torn or chewed the foot off. My friend purchased her, paid for treatment at a veterinarian's, and put her up for adoption. I volunteered to become the adopter, and since she still had the barred forehead feathers that signify a very young budgie, I decided to make her my first female parakeet student. To isolate the bird from her own kind for the initial lessons, I placed her in my bathroom, which was the only room in the house that did not have a bird in it. In so doing, I was breaking a fundamental rule of bird ownership: never keep a bird in the bathroom. In conformity with Murphy's Law, some day the cage door will be left open at the same time the toilet bowl is uncovered, and the bird will immediately plunge into it, jeopardizing the bird's safety. From the owner's point of view, since the only place in most bathrooms where a cage can be hung is the rod of the shower curtain, he will certainly bump his head on the cage's sharp corners and have difficulty keeping the overflow of seed and gravel out of the tub. On the other hand, the resonance afforded by the small enclosure makes a bathroom an excellent classroom, and I heard of one successful bird trainer who always placed her birds in the bathroom for their lessons. I named my new bird "Gilda" (in honor of the heroine in that day's opera broadcast of *Rigoletto*), hung the cage over the hook on the shower curtain rod, and thereafter developed such an obsession for closing toilet lids that I found myself shutting those at my friend's homes and even in the public buildings that offered such refinements in their restroom facilities!

But in spite of the excellent acoustics of my bathroom, Gilda remained aloof and unimpressed. Possibly the trauma associated with her accident made her suspicious of all human beings. After about six months I abandoned my efforts to educate her and put her in with the other parakeets which I kept in a large cage in my basement. Here she soon acquired a matronly appearance and, in spite of her handicap, more than held her own with the other females vying for the attention of the males.

Soon after Gilda became a "school dropout" a very slim white female found wandering in the neighborhood was brought to my bird haven. She, too, was quite wild, and with her first year—the one of greatest learning potential—behind her, I did not enroll her in my school. However, to isolate her from the other birds until I determined her state of health, I put her in a cage in my front room. When I returned home the next evening I found her comfortably ensconced on Snowball's swing, with Snowball himself squatting disconsolately in a corner of his cage. I repaired what I considered a weak spot in her own cage and put her back in it. The next night I found her in the cage of Mortimer the starling; she was perched cockily on the swing while Mortimer, obviously uncomfortable in his role as host, restlessly paced the floor of the cage. Either the mynah or the starling could have injured the parakeet. Fearing her next break-in would be pulled in the cage of Miss America the magpie, I put her in a finch cage with narrowly spaced bars which kept her confined until I introduced her to the other parakeets. Here she filled out nicely, her low-key profile evidently having been caused by her period of liberty, during which she obviously had dined neither often nor too well.

A few months later I was called to help capture a strikingly beautiful ice-blue female parakeet visiting a friend's bird feeder. Once in captivity she tested all points of her cage looking for a weak spot. When she could find no way to regain her freedom, she lapsed into listlessness. Even a roly-poly doll, a favorite with parakeets, failed to arouse any enthusiasm. Since neither Mrs. Ham nor I at that time was able to give her the attention it would have required to develop her latent potential, I gave her to Mrs. Curtis for a

Turquoisine grass
parakeets (left) are
not as common as
quaker or monk
parakeets (below).

A pair of Baraband superb parakeets; the more colorful bird is the male.

breeder, where her good looks would be passed on to future generations. As I set to work cleaning up the seeds and gravel in the bathtub underneath her cage, I reflected on the fact that getting a female parakeet to talk was a job for a real "pro."

A "pro" or "pro's"! A light suddenly dawned, and my glance automatically strayed to the red brick house across the street. With all of that bird-teaching talent next door going to waste, why should I involve myself in an exercise that netted me nothing but the job of cleaning birdseed out of my bathtub?

I phoned Mrs. Ham, informed her that the family would soon be the proud owners of a female parakeet and that I would pay a "fabulous" sum if they could both teach the bird to speak and record a few of its words. Then, without giving Mrs. Ham time either to accept or reject my offer, I was off to round up a candidate. Mrs. Curtis promptly produced a friendly green female which I purchased, put in my best cage, and introduced to the Hams. Great excitement reigned when it became evident the bird was enjoying the human attention as much as the family was enjoying her. Only the dog Tippy remained outside the circle of festivity; he went around with his head hanging, tail between his legs, sensing that this refugee from a badminton game was siphoning off some of the adulation formerly reserved for him. His mood was momentarily shared by Mrs. Ham when a disquieting thought occurred to her, and she asked me, apprehensively, "If we do get her to talk, then will you take her away from us?" Sensing a slowdown, if not a complete work stoppage, in the offing, I hastened to reply, "No, she is yours, and you can keep her regardless of what she does. Now start talking!"

And start talking they did, collectively, individually, in solo, in chorus, and I soon had a demonstration of what can be accomplished when real expertise is focused on a specific objective. The family commenced with the two easiest items for a bird to learn: the wolf whistle and "Pretty bird." The young lady was soon giving adequate versions of both, although her voice was very small and she included a good deal of gobbledygook in her efforts. Next came her name, "Juliet," which, after much debate with myself, I had selected with the devious reasoning that if she learned to say "Oh Romeo! Romeo!" it would be obvious to any knowledgeable listener that the bird was a female and her name was "Juliet." Juliet did eventually say both "Juliet" and "Romeo," frequently transposing syllables and thus re-titling Shakespeare's account of the immortal romance "Romiette and Julio." She also took artistic license with Waldteufel's "Skaters' Waltz," the tune played on her mus-ic box perch, liberally sprinkling her talking sessions with imitations of its tinkling notes. However, her favorite imita-tion of this particular instrument was of its less musical feature—the winding mechanism—which she ground out regularly with surprising volume.

In the six years Juliet has been an off-campus member of my educational facility, she has not become a distinguished linguist. Her imitations have favored nonhuman sounds, such as Tippy's bark and the tapping of typewriter keys, which she commenced soon after one of Karen Ham's late sessions typing a thesis. Her recordings, like her voice, are weak, but nevertheless they are proof that a female budgerigar can talk. Most owners of female budgies will agree, however, that their playfulness and personality are reasons enough for keeping them as pets. Any words they may pick up are only an extra bonus in the rewarding ex-perience of owning these peppy little playmates.

Lovebirds look like miniature parrots; a masked lovebird (above) and a peach-faced lovebird (facing page).

CHAPTER VIII

Polly Want a Cracker?

No book on talking birds would be complete without a separate chapter on parrots, THE talking birds in the minds of most people. Numerous stories, true and apocryphal, have been told about parrots. The first such true story I ever heard was related by my father, who had found his ability as a piano tuner a useful asset as he and my mother crossed Nebraska in a horse-drawn buggy in the early 1900's, enroute to their future home in Wyoming. In those days almost every farm family, however isolated, had a piano and welcomed the opportunity to have it put in listenable condition by the rare individuals passing through who were qualified to perform such a service. At that time the practice of locking doors was not as essential as it is today, and my father, according to his instructions from an absentee owner, entered an unlocked ranch house and prepared to tune the piano. When he struck the first chord a voice immediately said, "Stop that!" He looked around, but not seeing the speaker he went back to his work, only to receive the same arbitrary command a second time. Deciding to settle his status in the house at once, he began a search of the premises, and when he entered an adjoining room he was met by the solemn gaze of a big green parrot and the supplication, "Polly want a cracker!"

My father related another story which, in my youth, I accepted as fact but later realized he told with tongue-in-cheek. It concerned a preacher who would greet his parrot every morning with "Good morning, Polly, it's a very fine day," to which the parrot was supposed to answer, "Good morning, pastor, it's a very fine day." Unfortunately, the parrot was prone to say, "Good morning, pastor, it's a D--d fine day." After one such greeting the minister seized the cage by the ring in the top and whirled cage and occupant around his head several times; then he set the cage down and said blandly, "Good morning, Polly, it's a very fine day." With a bleary eye the parrot looked up and answered, "Good morning, pastor, it's a very fine day, but where in H--- were you when the cyclone went by?"

There are, however, enough true stories about parrots to entertain anyone without reaching into the realms of fancy. Owing to my late start in the field of talking birds, and with the astronomical prices reached for the best talking parrots, my personal experience with the large ones has been limited. When I retired, my office, wishing to assist me in my future work with talking birds, gave me a large enough collection to have purchased quite an expensive parrot. Knowing that I did not have either the time or the space necessary to give a valuable bird the attention required to develop its full potential, I opted instead for the relatively inexpensive monk or Quaker parakeet of Argentina. I selected a bald-headed little individual who looked as if he was getting the worst of it in a cage filled with these little green-and-gray birds and set up his headquarters on my front-room table.

I was looking for a suitably exotic name for my new bird which would indicate his Latin ancestry when Mrs. Curtis related an incident which settled my mind on a name for him. She said an elderly customer had come in recently with her parakeet named Kelly which she had purchased some years ago from Mrs. Curtis. The customer stated she was going into a nursing home where she could not keep her bird. When Mrs. Curtis picked up Kelly to determine his age by the date on his leg band, he quivered and died in her hand. The two women sat down and wept together. Since his leg band showed that he was about eight years old, it is likely Kelly would not have lived much longer

Many people believe that the African Grey parrot is the best talking parrot.

OPPOSITE:
Red-rumped parrots are rather small parrots; they have an enjoyable whistle, but their talking ability is uncertain.

anyway, but no one could blame his grieving owner for thinking he sensed they were to be separated and had no further wish to live. On hearing the story, I resolved that little Kelly should have a namesake and that my little green-and-gray bird would be it.

Monk parakeets can talk, but despite abundant companionship in the front room, Kelly never picked up any words. However, he became my official warning system, since from his position by the window he could see every person that passed the house. Whenever the screech which he uttered on such occasions was unduly extended and spiraled higher and higher in pitch, I knew someone had come up the steps and onto my porch.

My most valuable talking bird was, of course, Picklepuss the rose-breasted cockatoo, and I am ever grateful to the family that enabled me to add such a desirable bird to my collection. One day I entered a pet shop that featured exotic imported birds and noted a fine young female galah. "How much?" I asked the proprietor. "Two," he replied with a grin. I grinned back. I knew he meant $2,000, not $200. That evening when I passed Picklepuss's cage I put my face close to his bars and said, "How's my $2,000 baby?" He whipped his head around and neatly tatooed my nose with the dot-and-crescent which is the hallmark of the bite of a large parrot. It was as if he were saying, "It's not me you love; it's my price tag!"

But it was Mrs. Curtis's own parrots and the experiences she related about her customers' parrots which gave me my chief insight into the personalities and qualities of the large parrots. With nearly forty years of experience in the bird business, her recollections were endless. She told me about Silly Billy, a sulphur-crested cockatoo which she boarded for a year while his owner, an entertainer, wrangled with the authorities in her home state for permission to bring him back in after she had taken him on tour. This cockatoo was immortalized in Mrs. Curtis's memory for his ability to

DO-IT-YOURSELF RABBITEARS ADJUSTER
When I returned home late one evening and found my TV antenna on the floor, I feared an intruder "casing" my belongings might still be hiding in the house. But it turned out to be only an unlicensed TV repairman, Kelly the monk parakeet, making an unauthorized service call.

pick the lock on his cage and, keeping a low profile, move out into the pet supplies stacked along the sides of the shop, where he would, with one stroke of his beak, rip open a fifty-pound sack of bird seed and watch the contents fan out over the shop floor. Immortalized too in the memory of his owners must have been the half-moon parrot which, in addition to his daily bread, cost his owners seventy-nine cents a night, that being the price of a single wooden chew toy which he demolished nightly and without which he would squall the night away.

Rose-breasted cockatoos, or galahs, are popular partly because of their lovely coloring and partly because of their talking ability.

Long-billed corellas use their beaks to dig for food in the ground—and on trees!

Security Officer Major Macaw guards his companions.

Mrs. Anna Curtis with Cock Robin.

In addition to the many parrots she boarded or sold, Mrs. Curtis had a sizable battery of her own birds lined up in the back room of her shop, out of the public's eye. There was a big blue-and-gold macaw named Major stationed beside the entryway to this room, and only a very intrepid person would risk a chomp from Major's beak by attempting to pass the No Admittance sign. In this room she had, first, Connie, the nineteen-year-old Nanday conure, which had turned her back on the world and would eat only in complete privacy for a year after Mr. Curtis, her favorite, died. Next to her was Stone Face, an orange-cheeked Amazon whose name was descriptive of his demeanor. Then there were Cock Robin, a red-fronted Amazon whose pupils narrowed to pinpoints when any woman other than Mrs. Curtis approached him, and finally Pancho, a Mexican double yellow-head. Pancho's attitude toward me was "I'll let you alone if you'll let me alone," until one day I went into the back room wearing a hat. Pancho seized his favorite plaything, a wooden perch with one end chewed off and, with a meaningful glance in my direction, bit furiously at the perch, hammered it against the bottom of his cage, and glared at me again, emphasizing his point with frequent

87

The nanday conure is one of the more attractive conures; because of the coloring on its legs, some people say it has red silk stockings.

OPPOSITE:
Aside from having large beaks, macaws are also known for their loud voices! These are blue and gold macaws.

"Don't worry pal; you've still got me!"—Connie the conure gets comfort from a friend.

screeches. It was not hard to imagine that his ancestors might have watched voodoo rites in the jungle where effigies of fancied enemies are pricked and pounded by vengeful natives, supposedly transmitting unpleasant sensations to human counterparts.

Uncomplimentary as their reactions were, Cock Robin, Major, and Pancho at least took notice of their would-be admirers. But Stone Face did not grant a person the satisfaction of acknowledging one's presence at all. He merely stared impassively through a visitor as he continued to ponder the imponderables of life. Eventually, his attitude became mutual as far as I was concerned, and I came to take his presence for granted also.

Then one day when I went back to the parrots' quarters I was startled at the change in Stone Face. His facial feathers were ruffled, his eyes were attentive, he moved about in his cage freely, and he was so changed in attitude and appearance that I even asked, incredulously, if that was the same orange-cheek. Mrs. Curtis stated that of course it was, the change apparently being triggered when she moved Stone Face's cage close to Cock Robin's. "Those two have something going between them," she said, and since Cock Robin was known to be a male, undoubtedly Stone Face was a female. Previously, anyone would have been justified in assuming that the bird was sexless. I opined that if romance could unlock the coffers of personality in such a formerly unresponsive individual, then indeed the poets are correct in their assertion that "love makes the world go round."

This personality change made Stone Face a much more interesting bird, and for the first time it occurred to me to ask Mrs. Curtis about the orange-cheek's previous history. She said that she had ordered her twenty-five years ago for a young man from another state who was attending a local

Stone Face, an orange-cheeked Amazon.

Two blue-fronted Amazons—probably the most commonly available Amazon.

OPPOSITE:
Orange-winged Amazons generally have pleasing personalities .

university. He had asked her to keep the bird until he graduated, at which time he would pick it up and take it back to his home. But as the graduation date approached, the youth's sorrowing father came in and told Mrs. Curtis that his son had just been killed in an automobile accident. He said that although he and his wife knew how much the boy had looked forward to having the parrot, they could not bring themselves to keep it. Mrs. Curtis insisted on returning the lad's deposit, but said she could never bring herself to offer the bird for sale; she could not think of it as being anything but his bird. Consequently, Stone Face had found a happy home where she was valued highly and where, ultimately, she found her true self through the magic of love.

Fond as she was of her big and valuable birds, Mrs. Curtis was equally zealous and appreciative of the staple items in her trade, the parakeets. For many years she raised her own birds, and it was always a delight for me when she took me back in her aviary and, sliding half of the back panel off a breeding box, displayed a brood of squirming youngsters with their solicitous parents. In her late 70's Mrs. Curtis gave up breeding her own birds and began purchasing young parakeets from a friend in the business. However, she continued to keep the old breeders in large flight cages in her basement. Wanting such a cage for my increasing numbers of permanently disabled wild birds, I suggested that I give the old breeders in one of her cages smaller quarters in my own home, and I would take their cage and use it for my wild birds. At first she turned down my offer, but later, without enthusiasm, she agreed to such an exchange. Since I knew she was willing for me to have the cage, I was puzzled by her reluctance to part with these pensioners which were now nothing but a liability. When I visited her the day after the exchange, however, I found that she viewed them in a totally different light. "I hated to see those old birds leave here," she said wistfully. "They were the last of the flock that produced all those beautiful babies that put this shop on the map. They are old and decrepit now, but they were the beginnings of my prosperity." I realized that here was an unusual display of humility towards the lower animals. She was grateful to her livestock for services rendered which are ordinarily dismissed as only the tribute a superior is entitled to exact from an inferior. Human beings would be living at a higher ethical level if Mrs. Curtis's sensitivity towards the rest of creation was more universal.

Although man's affection for feathered pets is not as strong as it is for his four-footed friends, the dog and the cat, among birds the parrot tribe is the one most likely to call forth a comparable level of devotion. Highly intelligent and trainable (parrots are generally recognized as second only to the Corvidae in intelligence among birds), the Psittacine order contains members adapted to every range of taste and pocketbook. Two of the smallest, cleanest, most easily bred and, hence, least expensive of all parrot-type birds are the budgie and the cockatiel, which will always be among the most popular of cage birds. However, in spite of their escalation in price and their variability in temperament, the big parrots will always find champions for their cause and continue to inspire legends and stories as varied as the birds themselves.

Pied crows are fine mimics and can easily be taught to talk.

CHAPTER IX

Seven Crows a Secret

"If men had wings and bore black feathers, few of them would be clever enough to be crows."

Thus wrote Henry Ward Beecher, the famous abolitionist preacher of Civil War days and brother of Harriet Beecher Stowe, author of *Uncle Tom's Cabin.* This statement is an unusual comparison between man and the lower animals in that it is not wholly biased in man's favor. In my mind it established Reverend Beecher as the Patron Saint of crows, and I resolved that I would name my first crow after him. To keep my visions within the limits of reasonable expectations, I resolved to concentrate only upon the first name "Henry."

Henry the First arrived one spring evening when I answered the doorbell and found outside a railroad engineer friend who I knew had been visiting in Kansas. He had a big grin on his face and an even bigger box in his arms. When I opened it, a bewildered yet astute pair of shoe-button eyes set in a black, almost furry head, peered up out of its depths. My experience with a bird famed in fact and fiction for its intelligence and orneriness had begun.

I spent the rest of the time, until nearly midnight, making the new arrival comfortable and trying to provide him with nourishment, which he spit out as fast as I could thrust it into his beak. My night's sleep was disturbed by visions of making an emergency run to the veterinarian the next morning. However, when I explained the situation to my friend the next day, he assured me that the boys who had had the bird were old hands at taking care of crows and had warned him that the bird might be off its feed for a few days as the result of the long automobile ride and the change in its environment.

True to the boys' prediction, young Henry soon began to shape up and take an interest in his surroundings. I put him in a home-made wire cage in the same room with Audubon the mynah bird, who was at that time at the peak of his learning ability. Thus, I hoped the crow might pick up a few words from him. To some extent my hopes were realized; Henry eventually did give a basso version of Audubon's imitation of Mrs. Ham's laugh, a "Hi," and a not very acceptable version of "Henry," but enough to render token recognition of his model, Henry Ward Beecher.

Henry soon demonstrated by his flight pattern the accuracy of the expression "straight as the crow flies." It was evident he needed to flap straight forward in order to maintain flight speed. Although only half as large as the raven which I obtained a year or so later, Henry was deficient in the latter's maneuverability and made numerous "crash" landings when he ran out of flying space. Consequently he broke off the tips of his primary feathers and was unable to

"SCRAM!! Can't 'cha See I'm Taking A Shower ??"

fly at all for several months, although he would walk around in his room during his periods of liberty. When I was in the bathroom giving Audubon his bath in the washbasin, Henry frequently interrupted this intimate operation by entering the bathroom unannounced where, while watching the procedure from the floor, he soon learned to stand outside the periphery of the shower created by Audubon's flailing wings.

However, Audubon was not the only individual whose privacy was shattered by Henry's presence. The crow and Audubon were stationed in my spare bedroom and, while my house guests were few and far between, on one occasion out-of-town relatives elected to spend the night with me. They voiced no objection to sleeping with a crow, although I warned them that Henry had an annoying habit of uttering an endless series of "onk's" whenever he was hungry, and should they sleep beyond his normal breakfast time they might suffer a rude awakening. At the first "onk" the next morning I slipped into the room and placed a handful of dogmeal in Henry's tray. However, I noticed a very much awake eye peeking out of the bedclothes as I made my unobtrusive exit. Neither these guests nor any others overstayed their welcome, and I was unable to convince my office associates that I did not keep a crow in my spare bedroom to discourage lengthy stopovers at my house.

Henry had shared these quarters for over three years when an item appeared in his vocabulary whose origin was a mystery and which ultimately banished him to the garage. Without previous practice, he began to utter an extraordinarily loud "wow-wow-wow" which carried across the alley and halfway down the block. I could recall no dog which barked in that fashion, and I thought of the "wow-wow" sirens of emergency vehicles making their runs, except that these mechanical "wows" were run together in rapid succession in contrast to Henry's leisurely, strongly accented "wows." The crow's fondness for making this

REASON ENOUGH TO BE WORRIED:

I have just rescued Henry the crow from an attack by his powerful cousin Edgar, who, in the background, displays the massive profile characteristic of the raven.

sound was partly responsible for my decision to purchase the house next door when it came up for sale. The previous owners, two elderly sisters, had assured me none of the various sounds emanating from my property disturbed them, but I knew I could not count on new owners being equally tolerant.

Unfortunately, the raven in the next room was at his maximum learning stage. When I heard him practicing and producing, as befitted his stature, an even louder "wow," I knew that Henry would have to go; I could never endure "wow-wow-wow" in stereo. One morning, to the consternation of Audubon, I moved Henry to a back room in my garage already occupied by Mr. America the magpie, to whom Henry readily transferred his fraternal affections. My efforts, however, were too late to sidetrack the raven's interest in the "wow," and he soon came forth with a loud rendition which he uttered with the same enthusiasm and frequency as Henry. I closed the windows of Edgar's bedroom, having removed my own sleeping quarters to the basement, congratulated myself on my foresight in purchasing my second rental property, and resolved to counter any complaints from my tenants with the suggestion that they might be happier if they rented elsewhere.

No one complained, however, and in two years I sold the second property to a friend, also named Henry, whom I had known for half a century and who, with his wife, assured me they could endure any and all "wows" since they had a dog themselves.

Henry the crow had lived with Mr. America for two years when I received a call from a woman who had heard I owned a male crow. She informed me that the female crow she had owned for several years had recently begun to pull out her feathers, necessitating the installation of a plastic collar. The veterinarian whom she consulted ventured the opinion that the crow was lonely, and her feather-pulling could be alleviated only by companionship of her own kind.

101

My caller asked whether I would be willing to loan my crow for a trial period to see whether his company would soothe the female's ragged nerves. Believing that anyone who would incur the costs of veterinary expense would be equally solicitous of Henry's welfare, I agreed to her proposition. My new neighbor Henry went around with a very silly grin on his face when I informed him I was sending his namesake away to provide a little therapy for an emotionally disturbed old-maid crow. One fine spring morning I took my Henry across town to meet his new girlfriend. If the birds were all atwitter at this romantic interlude in their formerly humdrum lives, they kept their emotions well concealed, each gazing stolidly at the other from their separate cages. The owner of the female later reported that she put the two birds in the same cage, and the union seemed mutually agreeable, if not rapturous. From my standpoint, since Henry had passed the peak of his learning ability and since it requires a considerable amount of time, effort, and newspapers to keep a bird as large as a crow in captivity, the arrangement was particularly satisfactory. When I paid a visit to see how the newlyweds were making out, the owner was not at home, and four vociferous schipperke dogs, making up in enthusiasm for what they lacked in size, effectively discouraged me from inspecting the premises. A fervent and resounding "wow-wow" emanating from the shed assured me, however, that all was well in Honeymoon Cottage.

I am well aware that my five-year encounter with this one crow was not sufficient to do justice to either the talking potential of crows or their adaptability as pets. I have learned, both from observation of other people's pet crows and by correspondence, that crows have considerable ability for talking and, if given plenty of attention, are as companionable as dogs. A friend reported that in her childhood she knew a girl who had a pet crow which became a good talker and was devoted to his young owner. One summer the girl made an extended trip to California. Her crow promptly stopped eating and talking until, knowing how much their daughter cherished the bird, her parents phoned her that the crow was in dire straits. Although in those days travel was not so commonplace as it is today, and the trip was a highlight in her youthful experience, the girl cut her visit short. She returned home, to be greeted by her bird who ended both his hunger strike and his vow of silence when he heard her voice.

"One crow sorrow, two crows joy; three crows a wedding, four crows a boy; five crows silver, six crows gold, seven crows a secret never to be told" runs an old adage. Neither five years nor fifty are sufficient to learn everything there is to know about the crow or any other species of wildlife. Only to their Creator do the creatures of the wild reveal every facet of their nature. To humanity, some aspects of crows must forever remain "a secret never to be told."

The majestic raven—every inch a king!

CHAPTER X

Life with Edgar

It is said that when Edgar Allan Poe conceived the theme for the poem that would make him the godfather of all ravens from that time forward, he first thought of the parrot, which still symbolizes a talking bird in the minds of most people. But there is nothing malevolent or sinister about a parrot, even an ill-tempered one, and Poe was looking for a character that would embody all the somber overtones he wished to incorporate in his proposed poem. Somewhere in his experience, perhaps from reading Charles Dickens's *Barnaby Rudge*, in which a raven named Grips plays a prominent role, Poe knew that ravens can talk, and so he cast one as his harbinger of doom. He could not have hit upon a better candidate; throughout the temperate and northern climes which are its abode, the raven has been associated with the supernatural and regarded as an omen of ill-fortune—in short, a messenger from the Underworld.

And so Edgar Allan wrote his poem, which was accepted immediately in the English-speaking world as a work of literary art. Thus the raven, even though it spoke but one word, became fixed in the public eye as an outstanding talking bird. Actually, the raven does not equal the Indian hill mynahs, some of the large parrots, or the Australian budgerigar in speaking skills. However, no one has immortalized the achievements of these more gifted speakers in a work that has caught the public's fancy to the same degree as Poe's lines about the raven. Hence, it may be said that so far as literature is concerned, the raven is the most famous talking bird in the world.

Thus, as I progressed from one species to another in my

study of the talking birds, I came at last to the raven. Needless to say, in this phase of my study I knew in advance what the bird would be named and what the first word in its vocabulary must be.

The first order of business was to familiarize myself with the poem. Close reading immediately disclosed that, contrary to popular belief, the bird did not perch on the author's chamber door. He perched upon a bust of Pallas just above the chamber door. It was necessary, then, for me to research who "Pallas" was. In keeping with the eerie tone of the poem, I concluded Pallas must be of some importance in the Netherworld of mythology—like Pluto or Loki. Upon consulting the encyclopedia, however, I found that, in fact, my "he" was a "she" and that the name "Pallas" is linked with that of Athena—Pallas Athena, goddess of wisdom, war, the home, and other activities in Grecian legend. Since all the duties connected therewith are properly conducted in the light of day, "Pallas" has no threatening connotations that I know of, and it was never clear to me why Poe should insist the bird perch upon the bust rather than on some more level footing.

I broke off my contemplation of this facet of the poem to ponder another equally perplexing question: what was the architectural layout of Poe's chamber? The top of a door is normally among the highest nonstationary objects in a room. How or why a bust was mounted higher than the top of the door in this room was an unexplained mystery. I thought of transoms, which were popular in the high-ceilinged houses of that era, but, assuming the bird could or would fly into such narrow quarters, it would be very unlikely that the light could fall at such an angle as to cast the bird's shadow on the floor—and Poe makes it very clear in the last stanza of his poem that the raven's shadow did fall across the floor.

I concluded there are some things in poetry which are best left to the imagination and turned my attention to the very real problem of obtaining a young raven.

Ravens usually nest on inaccessible ledges or in the tops of the highest trees. They nest in the mountains of Colorado, but I had no mountain-climbing friends willing to go over a cliff on a rope, assuming a nest could be located. Besides, I could find no mention in my casualty insurance policy that coverage was provided for any person falling off a precipice while on an errand for me. While I was considering advertising for a raven and putting the burden for getting one on the shoulders of whoever answered my ad, I found just what I was looking for in a pet journal—an ad by a wild animal dealer that offered an assortment of young coyotes, bobcats, foxes, ravens, magpies, and crows. Early the next year I sent a deposit for a young male raven and received a notice the middle of the following June that one would be shipped on a certain date. After several phone calls to the air freight office on that day, I was informed by the clerk that my bird had just arrived. In a spirit of high adventure, I immediately took off for the airport to claim him. There was no doubt but that a whole new experience was opening up for me. In retrospect I have wondered whether, had I known all that experience would entail, I would have been so enthusiastic as I drove into the airport parking lot. At the counter I got enough of a view through the slats of the packing crate to see that it contained a live raven. While paying the transportation invoice, I explained to the clerk my purpose in buying such an unusual pet. He recalled, for my benefit, his one and only excursion into the education of talking birds, stating that he received one of the worst lickings of his life when his parents overheard him tutoring his grandma's parrot to say, "Hail, hail, the gang's all here; what the H--- do we care?"

Once in the car, my bird whimpered plaintively, and as I surveyed the container I realized that if the rest of his body was proportionately as large as his beak and what I could see of his head, he must be jampacked in there. In fact,

Get Thee Back into the Tempest and the Night's Plutonian Shore!—Judging from the model's reaction, Edgar Allan Poe did not overstate his case against having a raven perched upon one's chamber door.

when I began to take him out of the carton, I thought for a moment that the shipper had cut off his tail to pack him in the box. However, as he "unfolded," his tail gradually came into view, still intact and still attached—it had been bent back against his body during his travels in those cramped quarters. I realized, however, that the dealer was not necessarily hard-hearted in packing him in a box too small for him to move freely. With his movements restricted he could not hurt himself thrashing around in transit. Of course, had there been a delay enroute he would have been in real trouble, but as it was, even his tail appeared none the worse for wear.

I had prepared for him to be quartered in my own bedroom, having obtained beforehand a 4 x 4-foot portable dog cage and set it up on a pair of sawhorses. With the bowl of a bird bath for a drinking and bathing dish and a small iron frying pan for meal service, I felt I was offering accommodations fit for such an illustrious personage. As I placed him inside the cage I spoke the words that I later would say to him twice 10,000 times over: "Nevermore, Edgar, nevermore."

I decided to give him joint tenancy in my bedroom, a prospect that appalled even me. The decision was based, however, on the necessity of having him where he would get maximum exposure to my lessons, which could take place only mornings and evenings and week-ends since I was still working at my five-day-a-week job. Knowledgeable friends expressed doubt that such a bird could survive long indoors. I closed the furnace register in my bedroom, opened both windows, and hoped for the best. After a day or two to permit him to become accustomed to his new surroundings, I opened the cage door and watched Edgar make his first exploratory venture among the furnishings of my room. He hopped readily onto the wire threshold and soon spread his wings which, much against his will, Mrs. Ham and I had previously measured as over three feet across. He then sailed effortlessly into the 9 x 12 feet of freedom allotted him. His maneuverability was in striking contrast to the flight of Henry the crow, who had previously found the same space insufficient for him to maintain flying speed. It entails no small amount of control for a bird the size of a raven to launch himself and remain airborne in so small a space, but Edgar did it, making as wide an upsweeping curve as the walls permitted and landing on the top of his cage or on one of the three dressers in the room. However, I was not too much surprised at his achievement; ravens are among the world's best fliers, circling eagle-like, doing barrelrolls and doing stunts, apparently for the fun of it. They also play with light objects such as feathers or cigarette wrappers while in flight, passing them from beak to foot or dropping and retrieving them in flight. A friend who had spent time in Alaska reported watching this latter activity on a number of occasions, and Edgar soon gave me a demonstration of his instinctive propensity for holding objects with his feet. Lying late in bed one morning when Edgar was out of his cage and perching on the footboard of the bed, I heard a curious and continuing fluttering of his wings. Raising my head, I saw that he was standing on one foot, dangling a sheet of newspaper over the edge of the footboard with the other foot and maintaining his balance by a soft throbbing of his wings. He should not, of course, have been out of his cage at that hour, but I had not realized what it takes in the way of a lock to keep a raven confined in his cage. I had a large tongue-in-groove snap, commonly used to anchor tarpaulins and other heavy fabrics, which I snapped over wires in both the door and the frame of the cage, thus assuring, I thought, that he could not escape. But I had misjudged both the bird's intelligence and the strength of his jaws, for he soon found that by manipulating the snap into a certain position in his mandibles he could squeeze the tongue in far enough to slide the snap off both wires and gain his liberty. As a result, unless I remembered to wire the gate shut at night, I could expect a visitation from Edgar early the next morning. On one such occasion, just before dawn, I was aroused when I heard him fiddling with the snap; soon the rattling ceased, and there were two or three wingbeats and a soft jar as Edgar alighted on the footboard. Opening my eyes, I could barely make out his dark form silhouetted against the window that let in the rays of the slowly breaking morn. As I raised up on one elbow he arched his neck and flared out his shoulders, and in that posture he was truly a regal sight—every inch a king. A thrill of excitement surged through me as I realized that almost certainly I was the first person, in modern times at least, to see Poe's vision in reality—a live raven sitting, not on my chamber door, to be sure, but on an even more intimate object, my bed. A great moment, I felt, even though I was the only person to witness it.

But while my Edgar, in this instance, behaved in a manner suggesting his fictional counterpart, there were other ways in which his behavior bore no resemblance to that of the raven in literature. Poe's raven remained "put"—mine didn't. He would remain stationary only long enough to size up the situation and map his strategy. Invariably, he soon hopped down on the bed, and a tussle would ensue as to which one of us would "go." He would seek the highest point of the bedclothes—my knees or my feet—and pound vigorously. One Sunday morning when I attempted to lie abed and listen to my new tape recording of the opera *Daughter of the Regiment,* Edgar kept excellent time to its martial rhythms using my big toe, fortunately cushioned somewhat by the bedclothes, as a drum. I could not long endure his enthusiasm, however, and attempted to dislodge him with a kick from beneath the covers. But his capacity to absorb such upheavals was greater than the capacity of my leg to generate such kicks, and the contest ended with my being the one who abandoned the bed. On another occasion I also learned, before ending the experiment with a swift kick, that a raven's beak makes an excellent substitute for a doctor's rubber hammer in testing knee reflexes!

Yes, Edgar Allan Poe didn't know when he was well off. He would have had something to complain about had his raven ever gotten off that chamber door.

On another point, however, the two birds were in full agreement: both were persistent tappers, the only difference being that my Edgar's tapping could more accurately be termed pounding. I had replaced the tapestry rug in my bedroom with heavy asphalt linoleum. Soon Edgar pounded a hole through the linoleum which he subsequently enlarged at every opportunity. He next attacked a spot on the wall which he could reach through the bars of his cage, and he evidently put in much of his time hammering on the plaster while I was absent. I could not move his cage farther

Take Thy Beak From Out My Heart and Take Thy Form From Off My Door!

Quoth the raven: "*Nevermore!*"

away from the wall; already one drawer in the dresser next to his cage had been rendered inoperative by the protrusion of the cage into its pull-out space. Eventually, he enlarged the hole to such alarming proportions that I was reminded of Edgar Allan Poe's short story, "The Cask of Amontillado," in which an avenger walls up his enemy in a cavern in the family catacombs. Whether Edgar had any project like this in mind I do not know, but the hole finally became so large that anything he could carry might have been swallowed up in it. When in future years the house is torn down I wonder what may be found in the rubble under this particular wall.

Edgar Allan Poe makes it clear in the last stanza of his poem that he did not like the raven's shadow falling on the floor. Edgar the raven likewise had trouble with his own shadow but from just the opposite angle. During the summer months the sun shone through his window and reflected off the linoleum, and, especially when Edgar was sitting on top of his cage, it cast his shadow in reverse on the ceiling. Hearing cries of displeasure coming from his room one day, I went in and found Edgar angrily shadow-boxing with the apparition just a foot or two above his head. The more he leaped about, of course, the more activity he generated on the ceiling, and his quarrel with this elusive antagonist did not cease until the earth had moved in its inexorable course to where the sun's rays no longer created the annoying reflection. Edgar, in his own mind at least, was once again complete master of his premises.

On another point Edgar's behavior also digressed from that of Poe's raven. While the raven in the poem immediately chose for his permanent perch the door or the bust above it, my Edgar alighted on everything in the room except the top of the door. Possibly he was looking for a bust of Pallas to perch on. At any rate, it became evident that if I were to create, for a photograph, the spectacle of a raven perching on top of a door, I would have to bodily place Ed-

If you can't beat 'em, join 'em;
"Will you share my humble store?"

Quoth the raven: *"Forevermore!"*

gar on the door. I arranged for a friend to come over one evening with his camera and flash and, when he arrived, closed all doors opening into a hallway and placed the reluctant Edgar on top of a closet door. To add some realism to the setup, I asked Mr. Ham to sit on a chair in front of the door. The act did not begin or end as auspiciously as I had hoped. The camera flash, which had functioned perfectly on other occasions, fired only intermittently, so only a few of the pictures exposed turned out. Like Mortimer the starling, Edgar had no interest in starring in a famous scene in literature and looked in vain for an exit from his predicament. He was just as interested in what lay behind him as in what was in front of him, and he repeatedly flipped around, presenting his tail to the camera just as the flash went off. To keep him heading into the camera I went behind the door; this, however, was a mistake, because Edgar became more determined than ever to see that his rear guard was functioning. It was during one of these reversals that he had an "accident"—being naturally nervous and upset over these unaccustomed events—and Mr. Ham, seated in front of the door, was in the trajectory of the "missile." "It's hot," complained the unhappy target. "Maybe the bird's got a fever," giggled the irrepressible Mrs. Ham, as she went to the aid of her stricken husband.

Yes, Edgar Allan Poe's visitor behaved much differently than a real flesh-and-blood raven. Yet such was Poe's genius that through his imaginative pen the fictional raven has become, in the minds of millions of readers, the prototype by which all real-life ravens are judged. And is not this, after all, the mission of poetry and the gift of the poet: to transform the unreal into the real and lift the reader's thoughts from the everyday world to the higher levels of the imagination where even the creatures of the wild may step beyond the bounds of nature, and a raven may indeed enter the realm of man and contemplate the human condition, forevermore?

LOOK PRETTY, PLEASE!

Both pupil and teacher take time out to pose for a class photograph.

CHAPTER XI

The Education of Edgar

Man educates himself and other creatures basically for his own benefit. Rarely does training administered by a human being benefit any animal in the way of increasing its survival capability—the primary concern of all creatures living in the wild.

In no other type of education is man's self-interest more evident than in his preoccupation with training the lower animals to talk. Man's ego is flattered when he hears another form of life utter his own words. There is a great satisfaction in establishing such a rapport with a creature on a lower intellectual level. In no way, of course, does speech change the basic nature or intelligence of the animal which does learn to utter words, but subconsciously in the mind of man such a creature takes on a more human aspect.

I have used the term "lower animals" rather than "birds" in referring to talking species because, while the ability to imitate speech accurately is possessed only by certain species of birds, work has been done, reportedly with success, in getting somewhat human vocal responses from dogs, especially poodles. Similar efforts also have been expended on the higher apes, but so far man's closest relatives have been able to communicate with him only through sign language. Needless to say, my own interest in the subject was focused exclusively on the feathered clan.

While I was concerned primarily with training my birds to talk, there were other fields in which I would have liked to have imparted some training, particularly in the case of the more intelligent birds. There is a definite satisfaction in

HE'S SNEAKY! Here, Edgar lures Mrs. Ham within striking distance by placing his foot over his beak, seemingly immobilizing his most lethal weapon, only to make a lightning-quick stab when her hand comes within reach.

working with a bird of superior intelligence. One senses immediately a certain knowingness akin to his own feelings when working alongside an intelligent species such as the raven or crow. Perhaps it was my imagination, but I seemed to detect a cool, calculated appraisal of me in their shoebutton eyes, as if the birds were debating what they could do next to make life miserable for me to pay me back for having deprived them of their freedom. Whether intentional or not, the crow and the raven both succeeded in trying my patience to the maximum and creating literally mountains of paperwork for me or Mrs. Ham.

A situation in which any degree of education would have been an improvement was Edgar's treatment of the furnishings in my room. Since he had to have some opportunity to stretch his wings and exercise, and also because no bird can demonstrate all of its natural personality in a state of continuous captivity, I had to let him out of the cage for some time each day. During these intervals he reduced a plastic-covered hassock to a pile of excelsior. To protect the dresser and cabinet tops I covered them with a sheet of artificial leather and as extra protection piled newpapers on top of that. I discovered, too late to save the veneer on my dresser, that these measures were no protection against his powerful

118

beak. Newspapers he flung off the cabinets with reckless abandon, the bigger the pile the better. If he tired before he had pitched them all on the floor, the rest were soon blown off by the currents generated by his wingbeats.

To protect my bedding I purchased large strips of canvas, which I tucked in around the head and foot of the bed and along the sides. Even with these precautions I soon found that nothing can "unmake" a bed any faster than a raven; that he could not "make it up again" bothered Edgar not a whit. When winter set in, since I slept with the registers shut to assure that the room would not become too warm for him, I brought out a warm and snug family heirloom—a quilt filled with wool clipped from sheep on my great-grandfather's farm before the turn of the century. This became Edgar's favorite target, possibly because instinctively he associated wool, like hair or fur, as belonging to his natural food supply. He used this and whatever other bedclothes he could reach as a cupboard for storing food if I was so careless as to leave him out unsupervised. I learned early in the game that when I was letting him exercise it was preferable to offer him raisins or peanuts as snacks; when one has settled down for the night it is a much less traumatic experience to thrust one's toe into a cache of these edibles than into some more perishable substance!

It is this habit of the raven, shared by his relatives the jays, magpies, and crows, of hiding objects in crevices and other nooks that could have given rise to the story of ravens feeding the prophet Elijah in the desert. There is no doubt that if a person located a raven's cache he could retrieve an interesting array of "loot." Whether much of it would be edible by present-day standards would no doubt depend on how hungry a person might be.

I finally shifted my emphasis from protecting the bedclothes from his onslaughts to removing the temptation altogether, taking the bedclothes off the bed each morning and covering the mattress with papers and canvas. Eventually, of course, Edgar's diggings disclosed that a source of nearly inexhaustible goodies lay within the mattress, and I soon realized that when I no longer had a raven for a roommate one of my first purchases would be a new mattress. This happened after I had replaced the wool quilt with a feather comforter, and unknown to me, he got out into the room while the comforter was in place. Despite all my precautions, it was inevitable that one night I should fail to fasten the cage securely. That evening I watched the build-up of a full-fledged blizzard outdoors, unaware that in my bedroom Edgar was doing his "thing," using his bill as expertly as a seamstress would use a razor to open a seam in the quilt and create his own blizzard of feathers indoors.

But all of these frustrations were immaterial in the face of the more important lessons Edgar was destined to learn. My goal was to produce a recorded version of Edgar Allan Poe's poem with a real raven filling in the "Nevermore's." A raven's most frequently heard note in the wild is a croak, as distinguished from the "caw" of a crow, and while the literature on ravens credits them with a variety of other calls, none of it hints that the bird has any natural note that

resembles the word "Nevermore." My father was the only person I have known who believed that the raven actually does utter a version of "Nevermore." However, in describing the sound as he heard it, my father was very consistent in giving the word a peculiar inflection—"NEV-ermore." Riding his favorite horse amid the crags and canyons adjoining our ranch, he had an excellent opportunity to observe ravens in their natural element. Since he was a keen observer of nature, I could not write off his observation as a flight of fancy suggested by the poem. It appears, however, that Poe got his idea for the poem quite apart from any preconceived notion that the raven does say "Nevermore." By his own account, he first picked the word "Nevermore" and then structured his poem around it, the name "Lenore" presumably being chosen because it rhymed with "Nevermore." Contrary to some popular concepts, the poem was not written as a lament for his wife, whose name was Virginia and who, although in poor health, was very much alive at the time the poem was written.

In addition to "Nevermore" I also had hopes of getting the bird to say his name, Edgar Allan Poe. So as not to confuse him with too many words, however, I commenced with the phrase "Nevermore, Edgar, Nevermore." I said this to him over and over, the first thing in the morning and the last thing at night, strongly accenting the first syllable "NEV" in accordance with my father's rendition.

At that time I was renting my basement apartment to a young man who was attending the local university and whose bedroom was directly under mine. One evening when he came up to pay the rent I commented that I hoped Edgar's various squawks did not disturb him. My implied criticism of the bird's voice evidently struck the youth as inappropriate under the circumstances, for he replied courteously, "No, the bird doesn't bother me." Then he added casually, "But I will be glad when he learns to say 'Nevermore.'"

Smarting under this broad hint as to his rating of Edgar's voice with mine, I nevertheless continued my repetitious lessons, although now with a spirit of humility. By the time spring arrived there was no doubt that Edgar was exhibiting a flair for imitation. However, mixed in with his "Hi's" and "Hi-ya's," picked up from Mrs. Ham, was a curious exclamation that resembled the uneasy "Wuf" of an alert watchdog that senses something is amiss in his bailiwick. Presently, I noticed that this syllable was frequently associated with a second one that was unmistakably "More." I was overjoyed at this proof that Edgar was picking up the all-important word, but a disquieting suspicion entered my mind. Was it conceivable that my rendition of "NEVermore" actually sounded like that? There was one sure way to find out. It takes courage to hear ourselves as others hear us, no less than to "see ourselves as others see us," but I turned on the tape recorder and pronounced the word into the microphone with my accustomed vehemence. The playback left no question but that Edgar was giving a very good reproduction of what he—and my tenant downstairs—had been listening to for several months! I went back to pronouncing "Never" as uniformly as possible, and although Edgar never forgot the "NEV" or "Wuf," by Mother's Day of his second year he had recorded a very acceptable "Nevermore" for posterity. He was also doing a creditable version of "Edgar," albeit with a "grrr" at the end which sounded rather menacing but was, nevertheless, in agreement with the threatening overtones of the poem.

At this point I might mention that at the end of the school year my tenant decided to finish his schooling at a college a thousand miles away and moved out of my apartment. I have never heard from him since. In his mature years he will probably recall for the benefit of his grandchildren how, while studying for his degree, it was his luck to have for a landlady the only person in the world who was teaching a raven to say "Nevermore"!

But in spite of these embarrassments, I had achieved the goal that I had set; anything more Edgar might say would just be a bonus. I was, of course, interested in learning how extensive a vocabulary a raven can attain. A very natural thing for me to say to him was "Bad boy!" My experience with "NEV" should have taught me not to use any more special effects, but seeking to make the phrase more striking, I stretched out the word "baaad" in the manner frequently used by TV comedians. Shortly after I began concentrating on these words, I heard Edgar doing an excellent imitation of the bleating of a sheep or goat. He had never heard either animal in his life. This time I did not bother to check on myself with the tape recorder; I knew what Edgar was saying was undoubtedly a good imitation of my "baaad." Fortunately, he eventually completed the word with the "d," occasionally he shortened up on the "baa" part, and before the year was out I had a good recording of "You're a bad boy." In addition to the "wow" he had acquired from Henry the crow, he picked up the bark of my neighbor's Chihuahua named Tiny, and I hoped he would utter these two items at the appropriate time should an intruder ever seek access to my premises.

All in all, the education of Edgar was the most fascinating interlude in my entire association with talking birds. And since education is a two-way street, with teacher and student learning from each other, in terms of my own education my work with Edgar was certainly the most productive of my career.

As legend has it, a magpie's tongue must be split before the bird will talk—in fact, a magpie can talk without having its tongue split, though its vocabulary will probably not be as impressive as the bird's intelligence.

124

CHAPTER XII

There It Is in
Black and White

Of the "wild" birds available to people looking for a "talking" bird but unable or unwilling to obtain a parrot or a mynah, the magpie is the most colorful. Readily available in the western United States, the black-billed magpie, if obtained young and properly trained, is a good talker, with a loud "human" voice. A second species, the yellow-billed, is found only in the Central Valley of California and, because of its restricted range and hence rarity, it is less well known and under more rigid protection than the black-billed.

Since the black-billed magpie rarely ranges farther east than the high plains, many residents of the United States have never seen a wild one. Nevertheless, almost everyone, whether he has any personal knowledge of the bird or not, will quote the legend that a magpie's tongue must be split for it to talk. This superstition was passed down to the New World magpie from its European cousin, which it closely resembles. Thinking to do my part to lift the burden placed upon the species by this old wives' tale, I resolved that when I obtained a magpie the first phrase I would teach it would be: "Don't split my tongue."

A specimen was not long coming my way. My boss, who knew of my interest in the subject, announced one day in May that a neighbor boy had a young female magpie which must now be relocated since the family was moving from the state. He made an appointment for me to pick it up, but when I arrived, cage in hand, I found the male members of the family up on the garage roof trying to dislodge the fledgling, which had escaped while her young owner was taking her for a farewell stroll. For a few uncertain moments it appeared the bird would win the contest, but an expert catch in midair settled her fate, and she and I hastened home. I placed her in a large mynah cage which I reluctantly located in my kitchen, the only place remaining in the house where she would not be distracted by other birds. Thinking to give her a name incorporating strong syllables which might be easy for her to say, I called her "Hocus Pocus." My style-conscious cousin, who was visiting me at the time, took note of her smart ensemble of black and white and remarked critically that she didn't see as

"that name does a thing for her." A few days later, when I returned home, I found the bird had succeeded in unfastening the latch on her cage and was perched cockily on its top, looking as if she thought herself the finest thing in feathers. "Who do you think you are—Miss America?" I grumbled as I set out to dislodge her from the refuge she had sought on top of the kitchen door. My cousin agreed that this title was much more appropriate than the unimaginative "Hocus Pocus," and "Miss America" she became.

I began her lessons immediately. Thinking to drill her initially in something less complicated than "Don't split my tongue" and since the "itty" words seem to come easily to talking birds, I recorded "Pretty Girl" and "Naughty Boy" on a tape which I ran repeatedly. By her first Christmas she had learned these phrases, and by the following summer she had mastered "Don't split my———," "tongue" seeming to elude her, and I had to settle for something that sounded like "throat." Eventually, I incorporated her vocabulary into a skit with the Ham children which I played at programs to impress upon my audience the fallacy of the tongue-splitting tradition.

Meanwhile, a member of the bird club, learning of my magpie project, had called to ask if I would like to study the talking habits of a male black-billed magpie. Two young magpies had been orphaned when a farmer shot the parents, and she was attempting to farm them out to foster parents. Since my spare bedroom at that time was vacant, I accepted my friend's offer. However, Mr. America, as I decided to name him, showed little interest in becoming an orator. I therefore decided he might as well entertain me with the intelligence for which magpies are famous. For years I had admired the Oriental "bucketbirds," or great tits, related to our chickadees, which I had observed in pet shops, pulling up, foot over beak, small baskets baited with goodies. Mr. America was housed in a former "monkey cage" which was tall enough to accommodate a perch with

127

a receptacle suspended on a chain. I persuaded a neighbor to drill two holes in a small aluminum measuring cup and insert a wire bail. I then wired the cup to a chain, which I stapled to the perch in Mr. A.'s cage. I next put a bit of hamburger in the cup and retreated behind a door where, through the crack, I could observe his reaction to this setup. Mr. A. thoughtfully eyed the snack in the bucket below him, then jumped to the bottom of the cage, and, standing on tiptoe, deftly reached into the cup and snatched the tidbit. Wrathfully, I looped the chain half a turn over the perch, shortening it by about two inches, and again baited my trap. Once more Mr. A. studied the situation and then, apparently gauging correctly the distance as being too high for him to reach into the bucket from the bottom of the cage, he seized the chain in his beak and with a rapid foot-over-bill action maneuvered the bucket up to his perch almost too fast for me to follow the action. He gave several repeat performances until his hunger was satisfied, and I went back into the front room, congratulating myself on having obtained a natural-born bucketbird. Half an hour later I returned to find that I had a bird but no bucket; he had pried the bail out of the holes in the sides of the cup. I replaced the bail in the bucket intermittently over the next two days, at the end of which time he had pried the staple out of the perch and dismantled the whole contraption. I then took the assembly back to my neighbor; he replaced the bail with a longer wire which he twisted tightly into a handle, and then he screwed the upper end of the chain firmly into the perch. This arrangement proved to be very stable, and Mr. A. continued his performance at my plea-sure, often yanking the bucket up so violently that it flew over the perch and dumped the contents into the bottom of the cage.

When I acquired my crow, Henry Ward Beecher, I need-ed the cage for the new trainee. Since I knew I could not keep two such birds in the same room and get any talking

from them, I put Mr. A. in the choicest spot of all, from a bird's viewpoint: the big outdoor cage, where he could fly about with considerable liberty.

Since Miss A. had not learned any new phrases for nearly a year, I decided to give her a treat also and allow her male companionship. Before setting out for church one Sunday morning, I released her in the cage and then stood back to watch love blossom on first sight. Mr. A. promptly alighted alongside and tripped up to her so boldly that I could not help questioning whether his intentions were strictly honorable. Miss A. obviously recognized a wolf when she saw one and repulsed his advances with a well-placed peck. Her suitor moved away and tossed a few twigs about aimlessly, as if mulling over his next move. I suspected that a handsome "dog" like him would not give up easily. Still, I reflected, Miss A. was full grown and certainly able to take care of herself. I departed on my Sunday pilgrimage, feeling something like the debt-ridden father who abandons his virtuous daughter to the debonair villain who has the mortgage to the farm in his pocket and a leer on his lips.

When I returned home I went out to the cage and saw only Mr. A. walking about as if in search of his lost lady-love. I knew she could not have escaped from the cage, so I looked in the only blind spot in it—the space between its outer wire and the wooden side of a smaller cage that I kept inside the big one to confine small birds. There she was, wedged down in the crevice into which she had slipped but where her pursuer, somewhat larger, could not follow her. She had defended her honor to the limits that her environment permitted. Apologizing for having attempted to select a mate for her without her consent and convinced that if she preferred single blessedness to wedded bliss, I, a bachelor girl myself, should respect her wishes, I brought her back into my kitchen.

Eventually, I confined Mr. A. to a cage in my garage, along with other magpies and Henry the crow. In his second year he began to imitate the greetings of Karen Ham, who for a time took care of my outdoor birds. To my great satisfaction, later on he took notice of my lessons to the extent that he gave a very good version of "Don't split my tongue." Suzie Q, another female black-bill, also gave an acceptable account of the same phrase before escaping from my garage to freedom. Miss A., however, has been entirely content with her quarters in my kitchen and, although she

"No! No!
A Thousand Times, No!!"

Against the backdrop of the kitchen ceiling Miss America demonstrates the "form" whereby she won her title.

never acquired an extensive vocabulary, gave me my first success with the Corvidae and ushered in the most active and interesting period of my talking bird experiments.

What should be man's attitude towards the magpie, with its undeniable talent for mischief-making among domestic animals and its depredations among the game bird species in which man is particularly interested? "The bird is beautiful but it is evil," said a rancher when being interviewed on the subject. He was expressing an attitude which is all too common in the human race: Any creature whose activities may conflict with man's interests necessarily must be evil. Since *Homo sapiens* is, of all living things, the most vulnerable to charges of mistreatment of the lower animals, he is in the worst possible position to point the finger of guilt. Now that man has altered the chemical and physical composition of the out-of-doors to the detriment of the less adaptable forms of wildlife, there is the melancholy possibility that future generations will have to depend on the more intelligent and crafty birds for feathered companionship. Among this motley assemblage none will be more colorful, more interesting, and perhaps even more welcome than the magpie, many of whose traits and habits closely mirror those of man.

Green jays are attractive but noisy; their talking ability has not been established.

CHAPTER XIII
Tales of Sammy Jays

However unsophisticated the reading habits of the older generation may have been, they resulted in good memories cherished by those who were young in days when reading played a more important role as a pastime than it does today. A series of books popular among the small fry of the 1920's and 1930's was the Thornton W. Burgess *Bedtime Stories for Children.* Through the influence of Thornton's descriptive pen, Old Mother West Wind and her children, the Merry Little Breezes, along with the Smiling Pool and the Laughing Brook, became as real to their young readers as Charlotte and her web or the Flintstones are to today's TV viewers.

To a generation brought up on Walt Disney's *Bambi,* "Thumper" and "Flower" have become the standard names for rabbits and skunks. To those oldsters who were raised on the Burgess books, however, every skunk and every rabbit is still "Jimmy" and "Peter," who, through memory's eye, still frolic with their companions, Johnny Woodchuck, Little Joe Otter, and Sammy Jay, over the Green Meadows. As one of those who has such recollections, it was natural that when I began to entertain ideas of teaching a bluejay to talk there was no question but that my future pupil would be named "Sammy Jay."

But a Sammy Jay was not easy to come by. True to its reputation for secretiveness and alertness, no bluejay fell into the clutches of a cat or toppled at an untimely age from its nest until my bird rescue mission had been established for over a decade. Then one June day I received, quite literally, a windfall of Sammy's relatives. A young woman called saying that she had three baby bluejays which had tumbled from their nest in a high wind. She soon arrived with the tousled youngsters, crests erect. Only one was receptive to food, the others having to be force-fed for a day or two. When they stood up on their gangling legs, the heavy white feathering on their flanks made them look as if they were wearing the pantaloons favored by modest young ladies of an earlier day. The trio slept lined up on a perch, their heads turned back under the feathers between their wings. In that position, with the ring of dark feathers forming a border around the bluish gray patch on the nape of their necks, they resembled the back view of a line-up of tiny monks, heads shaven except for the dark ring of hair characteristic of some religious orders.

J. C. Rigli -
4-10-79

A few days after their arrival I was scheduled to meet a friend in southern Colorado and, since Mrs. Ham already had a load of baby birds to feed, I decided this would be a good opportunity to find out whether it was practicable to travel with a bird. I put the largest jay in a traveling cage, packed some of his rations in a compartment of my thermos jug, and set off, ready to prove that birds can be as satisfactory traveling companions as dogs. I placed Sammy and his cage in the back seat of the car; many accidents have been traced to the driver's attention being distracted by a pet in

Shock may result when any wild bird is forced to adapt to captivity. Here, a wild blue jay.

the front seat of a car, and I had no wish to be listed in the Courtesy Patrol's log as the first person to be involved in an auto accident caused by a bluejay. We had an enjoyable trip across the state, reaching our destination, Durango, about dusk. I gave Sammy a final feeding, covered his cage, rolled up the car windows, locked the car, and left Sammy for the night, not being certain that the rather excitable hotel manager would take kindly to a feathered guest.

The next morning when I went out and removed the cover from Sammy's cage, he greeted me with a weak squawk, toppled from his perch to the cage floor, and was dead within half an hour. Resolving never again to take so young a bird on a long trip or leave one unattended for any length of time, I left my little companion lying in a field of mountain bluebells whose color matched the azure of his wings. My friend and I drove on to get our individual problems into perspective by measuring them against a backdrop of the majestic San Juan Mountains.

Arriving home the evening of the next day, I was dismayed to find but one bluejay in the cage, and Mrs. Ham soon arrived to inform me that the previous morning—the same time that my bluejay had died 300 miles away—she had found one of the remaining two fledglings gasping its last on the floor of the cage. Although the young were not banded and we had not noticed any identification that would set one apart from the other, we suspected the survivor was the one which had accepted food and otherwise adapted to its new environment more readily.

I realized the death of the two jays might have been the result of shock. Adapting to such a radical change in lifestyle seemed difficult for the fledglings, and I spent the next few weeks sweating out the possibility that the remaining jay would go the way of his comrades. If he did, I would lose the entire year so far as my talking bird project was concerned, since he was the only new recruit. For about a month there was nothing in his attitude to encourage me in regard to the state of either his health or his morale. However, after six weeks his behavior took a turn for the better. He began to welcome me with soft chitterings and accepted my offerings of grapes and peanut halves with enthusiasm. Holding a peanut sliver between his feet, he would pound at it so vigorously with his beak that I feared I would soon have a bluejay with a perforated foot, his performance and its hazards resembling those at a woodchopping or railsplitting contest among humans.

A few weeks later, however, there was another change in his behavior, as if Mother Nature had switched his signals again. His response to my efforts to socialize or to educate him became erratic; he might greet me as his best friend on one entry and as his worst enemy the next. Any effort on my part to conduct normal activities in his room sent him into a panic, and I knew that any such disturbance lessened the likelihood that he would notice any of my carefully enunciated phrases. Therefore, I deferred moving for the

**TOO YOUNG TO WORRY ABOUT ANYTHING EXCEPT
"WHEN DO WE EAT?"**

Until they are from a week to ten days old, young of altricial species,
such as the nightingale above, have no sense of fear and will adapt to
any change in their environment. However, once the instinct of fear
has developed, many birds taken into captivity become victims of
stress—the inability of their nervous systems to adapt to a radical
change in their lifestyle. Many mysterious deaths among otherwise
healthy birds, adults as well as young, can be attributed to this cause.
Companionship of their own kind, or at least similar sized birds, is
sometimes, but not always, helpful in making the necessary
adjustment.

winter from my summer bedroom quarters in the basement
to my upstairs bedroom, where Sammy was located. Still, I
had to search my bureau drawers from time to time for
jewelry or other wearing apparel. Each search was treated
as a major crisis by Sammy, and I always ended up taking
the first article that came to hand and beating a hasty
retreat. "You little bum," I muttered on one of these occasions, casting a baleful glance in Sammy's direction. "Wait
until I have some of your imitations on record, and I will
show you who is boss!" But inwardly, of course, I knew
that any waiting to be done would be by me, not Sammy.

Exiled from my rightful quarters and denied the full use and enjoyment of my lawful property, I continued to sleep in the basement in the company of Picklepuss and his relatives. However, in October, on week-end mornings when I enjoyed the luxury of sleeping late, I noticed a wolf whistle coming from some undetermined point. I drowsily attributed the sound to Mortimer the starling upstairs, since he was the only member of my bird family that still uttered the whistle. However, one Saturday morning while I was combing my hair upstairs, I heard a loud whistle that came unmistakably from Sammy's room. Breakthrough! I was now one of the few people who had ever heard a bluejay imitate a human sound. Exultantly, I dashed to the kitchen, seized a grape, and hurried back to present it to Sammy, hoping he would associate the reward with his achievement. But a bluejay is ever alert to any change in familiar sights, and my half-combed hair hanging over my shoulders altered my appearance enough to represent, in Sammy's judgment, a threat to his continued well-being. Troubadours in the Age of Chivalry sang the more ardently when their lady-loves let down their flowing locks, but my streaming tresses only gave Sammy the screaming meemies. I hastily retreated, realizing I had not succeeded in impressing Sammy with the idea that the grape was a reward for his having whistled. It was a great source of satisfaction, however, for me to realize that I had, if not a talking bluejay, at least a whistling one.

Unfortunately for my project, Sammy's wolf whistle was his only contribution to my talking bird studies. During the ensuing fall and winter seasons he would drop it altogether, reinstating it in the spring so regularly that I came to regard Sammy's first wolf whistle, rather than the first robin, as the harbinger of spring. Since he gave me the "recognition display"—spreading his wings and vibrating his tail— which is characteristic of the male members of the Corvidae clan, I presumed him to be a male and that he elected to be the strong, silent type which is the privilege of the human male.

Another five years passed before a young jay of any species came my way. Then a friend in a nearby mountain town called to report she knew of a nest of a Steller's jay with ten-day-old young. Since Steller's jays usually build high up in an evergreen tree, I wondered how she knew the age of the youngsters, but she stated this pair of jays had built in a most unusual location—on the crossbeam inside a barn. On a drizzly day I drove the thirty miles to my friend's house with plenty of sunshine in my heart if not in the weather. Upon my arrival, my friend escorted me through the woods to the barn where, on the crossbeam about ten feet up, the bulky nest of sticks characteristic of most jays was located. She climbed a stepladder, found there were five young, and, with the permission of our hostess, brought down two of them. I placed my precious cargo in a basket padded with hay, and as I drove back down the canyon I told myself that my success with raising and training these little jays would be the measure of my professionalism.

There was no sunshine the next morning for me, either in or out-of-doors. Overanxious to get some food into the more backward of the babies, I pushed too large a mouthful into his beak, he gagged, and was dead within seconds. Obviously I was no candidate for the professional rating.

In addition to having to cope with an unfamiliar diet, the survivor was now faced with the additional hazard of stress induced by loss of contact with his kind. Memories of the fate of Sammy I's two siblings came back to haunt me. I could only offer such avian companionship as I had. On a corner of my front-room table I kept a grackle whose only contribution to my bird project was a raucous "Henry" picked up from Mortimer the starling. That grackle was, without doubt, for his size the most sloppy bird I ever possessed. But he would eat anything I offered him, from corn-

Thanks to their taste for an exotic location for a home, the pair of Steller's jays that built this nest enabled me to study the speaking habits of Sammy Steller.

flakes soaked in blackstrap molasses to cottage cheese mixed with pea soup. Anything that would savor my cooking and even come back for "seconds" was a friend indeed, and I had tolerated him for two years on my table for the pleasure of his company at mealtimes. I placed Sammy II in a box on the table beside the grackle, careful to put a cage over the box to make certain the grackle could not reach through the bars of his own cage and nip the little jay. Grackles are notorious for catching small birds, but I believed that, all opportunities for mischief eliminated, the grackle's dark silhouette would remind the jay of the outlines of his parents.

Later that morning I received a much-needed "break" when a young couple from across town enrolled a clamorous young robin in my nursery. I placed him in a cage on the other side of the jay, and when the robin went into his death-by-starvation act, the jay was sufficiently impressed by the little tragedian's performance that he began to implore food also. I kept a succession of young birds of various species in the jay's vicinity for the next two weeks, all of which did their bit in reminding him that one of the great pleasures in life is eating.

Within two weeks Sammy II had reached a sufficiently adult status that I felt the crisis was past, and not wishing him to become so accustomed to bird companionship that he would ignore human associates, I took him downstairs to my bedroom, where I placed him and his cage on the cedar chest beside my bed. In addition to my presence mornings and evenings he could also hear Snowball, Picklepuss, and Peter Pan. I had my cuckoo clock repaired and kept it running, hoping its frequent ejaculations might catch Sammy's attention, and I also placed the phone on the cedar chest beside his cage, thinking its ring might prove of interest to him.

When Sammy II was about seven weeks old, two tiny spots of white pinfeathers appeared on his forehead at the

SQUEAKY THE GRACKLE—

the only living creature, including me, who enjoyed my cooking!

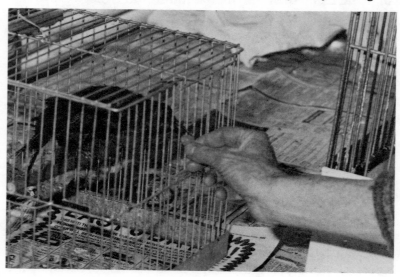

base of his bill. They were the beginning of the famous pair of double white eyebrows that decorate the head of the adult Steller's jay. I was so interested in watching their growth that I did not notice, at first, the less conspicuous white streaks that grew in at the same time just above his eyes. He eventually molted all of his head feathers, including the famous crest that has earned the Steller's jay its alternate name, "long-crested jay." Unlike the starling, which within a few weeks after leaving the nest undergoes a complete molt into the adult plumage, the fledgling jays have the full suits of the adults except for their "helmets." Apparently, the striking head pattern is essential for a Steller's jay to operate among his kind as an adult.

Meanwhile, a very babyish young bluejay trying to escape the attentions of an inquisitive dog in a nearby backyard reached my rescue mission. I regarded his arrival as double "insurance" on the success of my bluejay experiments and placed him, reluctantly, in the last room of my house which was birdless: my bathroom. I reactivated my phobia against open toilet bowls, put papers down in the bathtub to keep falling debris from plugging the drain, and commenced my lessons with "You're a pretty, pretty baby" and "Whatcha-doin', Cupcake?" In saying these phrases to him I was using sounds that almost any bird will say, if he is going to talk at all: pretty, ura, whatcha-doin', and the consonant *K*.

The arrival of the bluejay, of course, called for some adjustment in nomenclature. To avoid confusion, I transferred the name "Sammy II" from the Steller's to the bluejay and referred thereafter to my first jay as Sammy Steller. Naturally, I used the opportunity to compare the behavior of the two cousins. Sammy Steller was much the more active of the two, constantly bounding about in his cage and regarding me with curiosity rather than friendliness. In contrast, while Sammy II, like all of the Corvidae, was smart enough to take anything people said or did "with a grain of salt," he retained an element of immaturity, begging for food with fluttering wings and regarding me with much more trust than the Steller's. His crest was never raised unless he was perturbed, whereas Sammy Steller's crest was almost always raised, waving as jauntily as the banner of a knight riding forth to a tournament. Like Sammy Steller, the bluejay molted his head feathers at eight or nine weeks of age, although I did not notice a pronounced pattern change when he attained his new headdress. Both birds were equally messy. The motto of Sammy II was apparently "Cleanliness is next to godliness," for he took a bath immediately after every change of his water and his cage papers. Sammy Steller appeared to labor under the delusion that his cage contained buried treasure and spent much of his time rummaging for it amid his floor papers. Like my other jays, both were content with a diet of soaked dogfood, unsalted soda crackers, peanuts, and grapes.

By September Sammy Steller was vocalizing every morning when I left his cage covered for what he evidently considered too long a time. That he was giving imitations of various sounds was evident; unfortunately, he showed a preference for noises of which I already had too many. He gave such excellent imitations of the screeches of Peter Pan and Greenjeans that both birds frequently answered him from the next room. However, he also imitated the "sit right down" call of the female of my pair of painted quail. This was the rarest sound in my aviary. Of the thousands of feet of magnetic tape I ran off trying to get acceptable versions of offerings by the various birds in my basement, only once did the quail notes get on the tape. The pair sat together on the floor of the cage at night, but apparently when one bird strayed from the other's side, the female would give her sharp contact call. Since, in spite of its rarity, this became Sammy's favorite imitation, I concluded such pinched, astringent sounds may appeal to birds that mimic. The notes of killdeer, which are of the same sharp quality,

144

Sammy Steller's favorite voice models were painted quail.

are favorite imitations by the starling. Sammy Steller also picked up snatches of Peter Pan's whistling, which he soon converted to the conventional wolf whistle, a sound that evidently comes easy to jays. In addition he picked up an excellent "cough." Unfortunately, my own carefully enunciated lessons had fallen on deaf ears. But I set up my tape recorder and recorded such sounds as he had learned, and with proof that a Steller's jay can, indeed, give imitations, I could only await future developments.

When January arrived, with its unpaid bills and warnings of tax deadlines, I was reminded that my jays were also approaching a deadline—the end of their first year and the period during which a bird is most likely to learn some words. In an effort to salvage some rewards for the inconveniences I had experienced with a jay in the bathroom and another on my immobilized cedar chest, I redoubled my efforts to secure some comments from my jays. I decided to concentrate my personal attention on Sammy II, reasoning

Although painted quail obviously incubate their eggs in the wild, in captivity they are erratic "sitters." Here a female quail dutifully performs her maternal duties.

that if Sammy Steller was not impressed by any of the voices he could hear in his room, he would not be responsive to my own. From the bedroom above him, Edgar's voice was doubtless as audible to Sammy as it had been to my late roomer, while from the adjacent room there was conversation from Picklepuss, Snowball, Peter Pan, and even Greenjeans, whose principal contribution to the discussion, "You're a stinkpot!" was something I wished I had never said to the insolent little hussy.

For Sammy II, in the upstairs bathroom, I invested my best personal efforts. Since a bathroom is hardly a stimulating environment for any bird, I tried to think of ways to entertain him while I was in it. Sammy's night life really began at about 10 p.m., at which time I usually began my preparations for bed. For Sammy, the highlight of the floor

146

show was my teeth cleaning ritual. He was particularly intrigued by my toothbrush and, one evening, to further his interest, I held it close to his cage for his inspection. Too close, it turned out, because he suddenly shoved his beak through the bars and momentarily gripped the bristles. However, his reaction to the toothpaste still saturating the bristles and his efforts to remove all traces of the offending substance from his beak convinced me that birds are fortunate there is no such thing as "hen's teeth." Although I later held the brush up at a more discreet distance, he never attempted to grasp it. Apparently, his memory was long enough to prevent him from making the same mistake twice. He still liked to play with the wedge-shaped toothpick with which I concluded the ceremonies, and he fidgeted in his cage until, after washing off the taint of surplus toothpaste, I presented it to him.

Joseph C. Rigli-
12-13-78

Greenjeans, super schoolmarm (above), and her pupil, Sammy Steller (below).

But the grand finale of my performance, and the one which Sammy felt warranted audience participation, was my bath. Since he was more alert in the morning and hence more vocal, I frequently deferred this operation until morning. The sound of running and splashing water seemed to appeal to him, so I extended my ablutions as long as possible so as to monitor his complete performance. It was indeed during one of these soaking sessions that I learned Sammy was giving what turned out to be his one and only imitation, the incessant rik-rak-zip-zap chattering of Kelly, the monk parakeet, in the front room.

While Sammy II occupied my attention at the close of the day, Sammy Steller had his turn during the early morning hours. I found that if I lay abed late enough he would amuse himself by going through his full repertoire. During one such lazy session Sammy Steller rewarded me with another red-letter occasion—the moment when I heard, for the first time, the "speaking voice" of a new species. He gave the cockatiel screech and Peter answered him. He squawked like Greenjeans, whistled and coughed; then suddenly he gave an unmistakable and loud "come back," a favorite phrase with Greenjeans. A "come back" of sorts is among the natural calls of the canary-winged parakeet, but Greenjeans had refined her rendition by repeated lessons from Mrs. Ham, who stood before the cage bobbing her head and exclaiming "Please come back!" I turned on my tape recorder every morning after that and finally Sammy went on record as a speaking Steller's jay. Admittedly, Sammy's achievement was strictly "second-hand," using Greenjean's voice rather than a human's. Though I spent considerable time running tape recordings in an attempt to elicit other imitations, neither jay gave me further successes.

Had it not been for Greenjeans, of course, I would have had to admit that I "struck out" three times. This poor batting average undoubtedly resulted mainly from my own in-

"Of course I do have a roof over my head and three square meals a day, but no privacy—even my 'cell' is bugged!"

eptness as a trainer and the humdrum environment in which my jays spent most of their time. However, making full allowance for such lack of motivation, I believe it is safe to say that jays are, at best, unpredictable performers. Certainly, they do not have the aptitude possessed by their cousins, the magpies, for imitating the human voice. I have known of two pet bluejays that, like Sammy I, never gave anything but the wolf whistle. However, one of my correspondents reported that during a vacation in the Redwoods of California, he stayed at a small cottage camp where the owner, an elderly man, had accomplished the unusual feat of taming a number of wild Steller's jays to eat out of his hand. My informant soon noted that one of the birds uttered an unusual call, and when his host gave him a clue, he realized that the bird was saying "Jaybird." Only the one bird said it. This incident reveals the odds against which the student of this facet of bird behavior must work: mat-

150

ching the receptive bird with the accepted trainer is a matter of sheer chance.

With the modest achievements of Sammy Steller, I closed the official part of my talking bird study. I retired from the field not, as in the case of Alexander the Great, because I felt there were no more worlds to conquer, but because with a bird cage on every table and dresser in my house and the number of permanent pensioners growing at an alarming pace, I had no time to do anything except feed, train, and record birds. There are abundant opportunities and thrills still awaiting anyone who chooses to investigate further this provocative subject. I can wish future experimenters nothing more than that their lives may be enriched as much as mine has been by the personalities, antics, foibles, and accomplishments of the talking birds.

House sparrows have reportedly chirped in a manner close to human speech, but actual "spoken" words have not been recorded.

CHAPTER XIV

What About the Others?

I had my big moment in the public spotlight one summer when a local newspaper, in accordance with its custom of occasionally highlighting items of a more relaxing nature, printed my picture on the front page and referred to me as the "Bird Lady of Denver." I told my friends that having reached the zenith of my career, there was no way for me to go but down. This prediction came true sooner than I expected. As part of this same article there was a picture story showing me and some of my talking birds with the title "They All Talk." Soon afterwards, a friend sent me a copy of a newspaper from another part of the state which contained a condensation of the original article under the title "Bird Lady of Denver Says All Birds Can Be Taught To Talk." I had not made, of course, any such rash statement, and I thus joined the throngs of people, famous and otherwise, who complain that they have been misquoted.

Quite the opposite of the above headline is true. Worldwide, the most outstanding talking birds belong to only three groups: the order Psittaciformes, which covers the parrots and parrot-type birds, and two families of the Passeriformes order: the Sturnidae, which includes the mynahs and starlings, and the Corvidae, or raven-crow-magpie-jay complex.

There are about three hundred and fifteen members of the Psittaciformes order; over one hundred in the Corvidae family, which is sometimes extended to cover the birds of paradise, bowerbirds, and drongos; and approximately one hundred and six in the Sturnidae family. Information on the talking ability of the five hundred species represented

Jackdaws are one of the members of the family Corvidae known to talk.

in these groups is spotty. Talking has been documented on the more common members of the Old World Corvidae, such as the jackdaw, hooded and carrion crows, rook, chough, raven, magpie, and jay. A British correspondent reports that he purchased, from a Finnish sailor, a young Siberian jay, related to the famous camprobber of North America, which learned some words but was not as accomplished a talker as a European jay. Some authorities believe that under favorable circumstances any of the hook-bills, or parrot types, can talk. The same statement might be applicable also to the other two groups, but many of the species are so rare or reside in such remote areas that little is known of their habits in general, much less of their talking ability. In remote villages throughout the world there may be individuals of many species which have been kept as pets and thus may have picked up some words in the local tongue, but such records have little chance of reaching the outside world. What can be said for a certainty is that each of the above three groups contains species which have consistently proven their talking ability.

However, "talking" is only the extension into human vocabularies of the propensity of certain birds to mimic sounds. Every continent, except perhaps the Antarctic, contains many species that are excellent mimics, usually of the sounds made by other birds. Curiously enough, the two most accomplished mimickers—the mockingbird of the Western Hemisphere and the lyrebird of Australia—rarely include human sounds in their repertoire even when they have been in contact with human voices. I have uncovered only one authentic report of a mockingbird that talked. This was a wild one that occasionally said "Edward." The mocker's territory included property owned by a man whose first name was Edward. Apparently, Edward's wife called him often enough that the bird picked up the word. There is, however, a report of a brown thrasher, a relative of the mockingbird, that did considerable human vocalizing.

An Australian correspondent has advised me that he believes human speech does not have sufficient volume to attract the attention of the lyrebird. However, I read one item concerning a lyrebird that did repeat human sounds which, in the circumstances, were probably of the required volume. A rancher and one of his workmen were digging post holes in lyrebird country when the employee pounded his toe. The poor fellow naturally expressed his anguish vocally. When his cries were unduly prolonged, however, his employer called across to him saying, "Surely your foot can't hurt that bad after all this time," whereupon the workman replied, "That's not me; that's the bird." It would have been of interest for my purposes if the writer could have reported whether the workman used some "cuss words" in his tirade and if these were included in the lyrebird's account of the event as well.

An authority at one of the large zoos informs me that besides the Psittacidae, Sturnidae, and Corvidae mentioned above, theoretically, at least, the bell magpies of Australia, which are not related to the magpies of Europe and North America, and even some of the birds of paradise may be capable of imitating human speech. There is an early account of an Australian butcherbird and a bell magpie that did talk, and my Australian correspondent states he knows of several that have whistled tunes. Since the birds of paradise are related to the crow, it would seem logical that they might be able to pick up words. I envy the lucky individual who, in the future, may have the opportunity to cultivate a speaking acquaintance with some of these exotic birds.

However, it is possible that any species of bird that imitates may contain individuals that would imitate the human voice if kept in captivity. Occasionally, some of these gifted individuals do surface. I was told of a captive European bullfinch, a species famous for whistling tunes, that also talked. I have read one statement that some of the African whydahs or "widowbirds" can talk. From England comes a report of a house sparrow that chirped in a cadence that resembled human speech. There are reports from both the United States and Europe of at least three canaries that talked well enough to be understood. Mrs. E.L. Moon, an authority on cockatiels and other cage birds, reported a tame bobwhite quail uttered several sounds that were recognizable to her and visitors as "Talk, talk, whip-poor-will" and must have been deliberate imitations, although this is the only instance I have heard of gallinaceous birds giving imitations.

One of the most unexpected candidates for speaking honors uncovered in research for this chapter is the family of New World blackbirds, or Icteridae, which, to my knowledge, have never had a reputation for imitating anything. My first inkling of blackbirds' ability to talk was a report that a caged Brewer's blackbird in Oregon said a few words. This news was so unusual that I wrote the owner, who confirmed the report and stated I would be welcome to record the bird; unfortunately, I was never able to make the 1500-mile trip. Later, a correspondent in California sent me an article written in the 1930's concerning several cap-

Brown thrashers can evidently learn human speech as well as, if not better than, mockingbirds.

tive male red-winged blackbirds which were even better talkers than their classmates the bluejays. Female redwings, the article stated, did not talk. The same correspondent later sent me a report of still another male redwing that sang like a cardinal and crowed like a bantam rooster. The new vistas opened by this information made me regret that a young male red-winged blackbird, a common bird in my area, had not reached my nursery in time for me to have included it in my study.

The family Turdidae includes thrushes and thrush-like birds, some of which, in addition to being among the world's finest songsters, are known to mimic other birds and human whistling and thus might also talk. One of these is the shama thrush, an individual which, in captivity, was observed imitating his roommate, a talking cockatiel. There is also an early report of a tame European blue rock thrush that said, very clearly, "Pretty bird."

But I suspect that the preceding discussion and speculation as to possible talking birds might not satisfy the staff member on that newspaper who extended my headline to state that all birds can talk. "Why," he or she might ask, "*don't* all birds talk?" It is true that all birds have the same basic vocal equipment, that is, trachea, bronchi, syrinx, air sacs, and larynx. Development of this equipment, however, varies in different species. One bird related to the birds of paradise is called "trumpet bird" because of its extraordinarily loud call made possible by its greatly elongated trachea which is actually coiled several times within the body cavity. In some species, such as ducks, the syrinx is hardened into a bony drum which may preclude any extensive vocalizing. The placement and size of air sacs, necessary for resonance and amplification, also vary among species.

But perhaps most important for the extension of avian vocalization into the realm of imitation of any kind may be the intricate factors involved in a bird's nervous system. This is what limits the ability of the higher apes to use human speech. The gorilla, as I am told, has the same basic vocal equipment as man, including vocal cords, larynx, sinus cavities, and tongue, but the nerve pattern which connects the vocal equipment to the brain and, of course, the development of the brain itself are markedly different from those of man. Thus, while the gorilla has the intelligence to converse by means of sign language with human researchers, it is unable to learn the speech that would convey the same message vocally. Likewise, it is probable that most birds lack the "wiring" that would enable them to imitate any sounds, including human speech.

However, variability in vocal equipment and intelligence cannot explain all of the questions involved in the phenomenon of imitation among birds. Intelligence might help explain why crows, ravens, magpies, and some parrots, whose natural cries are raucous and guttural, can use their apparently inferior vocal equipment to produce human sounds while other species with equally primitive voices cannot. Nevertheless, equally intelligent members of the

Shama thrushes are songsters as well as mimics of things musical—human whistling, for example.

same family do not perform equally well. African gray and yellow-naped parrots are better talkers than are the cockatoos and macaws, which are intelligent enough to learn complicated tricks. Likewise, African lovebirds, which are better performers in avian circuses than the garrulous Australian grass parakeets, seldom imitate their master's voice. Neither is there any satisfactory explanation of why the greater Indian hill and Java mynahs are almost compulsive talkers while the common mynah and many other relatives are not. Answers to these questions are probably as elusive as an explanation of why some human beings are gifted with musical or artistic talent while others are not. The talking birds do not give up their secrets easily. There are enough unanswered questions in this area to occupy researchers for as long as man's curiosity persists about the creatures that share this globe with him.

CHAPTER XV
Getting Them to Talk

"Talk is cheap" runs a popular proverb. "Words, words, words," scoffs Hamlet, indicating that words are of themselves unimportant. But to any person who has his heart set on hearing a bird repeat his own words, neither of the above attitudes conveys the amount of time and frustration that may go into making that dream come true. Far from being cheap, sometimes it seems that, word for word, a talking bird commands as high a fee for his dictums as a doctor, lawyer, or any other person of comparable professional stature.

Even so, the person who achieves this goal will affirm that the effort is worthwhile. Surely one of the most innocent, satisfying, and unspoiled sources of human pleasure, dropped perhaps as an afterthought by a kind Providence into this vale of trial and toil, is the propensity of certain species of birds to imitate the human voice. As previously mentioned, there is a distinction between this ability or inclination of certain birds to mimic human speech as opposed to other forms of imitation.

All vocal sounds, including "words," produced by a bird emanate from the syrinx. This is an organ located at the lower end of the "windpipe" or trachea which controls, with a complicated set of muscles, two membranes, one in each bronchial tube. A bird also possesses a larynx located, as in man, at the upper end of the trachea, which, while not used for producing sounds as is the "Adam's apple" in man, probably does contribute to the resonance or amplification necessary for sounds produced in the syrinx to become audible.

160

Australian butcherbirds (right) and bell magpies (below) have been "caught" whistling tunes and talking.

Contrary to human speech, a bird's tongue has little, if anything, to do with the formation of words. I have heard Miss America and Edgar utter words with their beaks so full of food—and, in Picklepuss's case, half a clothespin—that the tongue could not possibly have been in action. The superstition that any bird's tongue must be split or "freed" to enable it to talk is but a glaring example of man's arrogance in assuming Nature can do nothing right without an "assist" from him.

So much for the vocal equipment which enables birds, in addition to voicing their own natural vocabulary, to imitate human speech. How does one persuade them to use this equipment for the edification of their owners? I use the word "persuade" because this is what man must do if he would hear his words reproduced by birds. They cannot be forced, coerced, frightened, intimidated, or bribed to exercise this unique ability; their imitation of the human voice is a free-will offering bestowed only on those owners who have won their confidence and total acceptance. Once bird and owner have reached that common ground and the bird has begun to imitate, it will likely be "hooked" on sounds and repeat whatever attracts its attention throughout its learning span or even its lifetime. The learning span varies among species. The first year is the most productive period, since this is the time during which the bird would be learning its native language in the wild. The mynahs have a comparatively short learning span, about a year and a half, although a patient and persistent trainer may prolong this period with intensive training sessions. Individuals in the parrot family can continue to learn new phrases that interest them for an indefinite period; the owner of a twenty-year-old African gray parrot reported that the bird still picked up new phrases. The key to what a bird will learn and how long it retains it undoubtedly lies in what happens to appeal to the bird. My Mortimer starling had learned nothing new since his third year, but in his ninth year became intrigued by the "ha-ha-ha" call of a new magpie I brought into the front room. He speedily perfected his imitation of it and thereafter made it his favorite vocal exercise. Although Miss America had been within hearing distance all his life, he had never been exposed to this natural note; she virtually never uttered any of a magpie's normal repertoire.

How, then, does one get a bird to talk? The popular idea is that if a person buys a parrot, mynah, or parakeet and repeats a phrase for a few days the bird will automatically learn it and ever after be a linguist whose ability will be available at the owner's pleasure. I knew of a man who, intrigued by the spectacular talking ability of a budgie belonging to a woman acquaintance, offered her fifty dollars, a large sum at the time, if she would train such a bird for him. A storekeeper whose safe was cracked one night told news reporters he was confident his parrot, which occupied the room in which the safe was located, would eventually state the name of the thief.

It is doubtful if either bird would perform in accordance with the above scenarios. Birds have to be "reminded" of their human utterances periodically or they will gradually drop them, and the budgie, accustomed to a woman's voice, would probably soon lose much of the repertoire for which the man had paid the fifty dollars. As for the parrot in the burglarized store, he certainly would not repeat the name of any person he had not heard greeted often by name, and it is unlikely any such long-time acquaintance conducted the robbery in the first place. As is the case with everything else in Nature, the talking birds operate under their own set of rules, and human beings must conform to those rules if they hope to capitalize on any bird's ability to talk.

People ask, "Can you tell by looking at a bird before you buy it whether it will talk?" I would say you cannot tell by looking at a bird whether it will talk any more than the bird can tell by looking at you whether you will make a good

Mockingbirds are known for being great mimics but not for including speech in their mimicry.

OPPOSITE:
Lyrebirds are as famous for their mimicry
as mockingbirds, but reports of lyrebirds
imitating speech are as rare as those of
mockingbirds.

164

master! Patronize a reputable dealer, be sure the bird you are purchasing is young and healthy, and then have faith in both the bird and yourself. Always keep in mind that regardless of how much talent your bird may possess, his performance as a linguist will depend largely on your performance as a trainer.

What, then, are the qualifications of a good bird trainer? Patience, enthusiasm, and persistence. With these characteristics any person can teach a bird to say something. However, I cannot escape the conclusion that some people produce better "vibes" in birds than others—Mrs. Ham vs. me, for instance! Birds also show an affinity for children. When several small youngsters walked into Audubon's room he greeted them with a liberal assortment of his vocabulary; shortly thereafter, when a set of oldsters called on him, he remained mum, subjecting them to the piercing scrutiny that is characteristic of mynahs.

A striking example of the bond between the very young and birds was related in a pet magazine. A vicious parrot had proven on several occasions he was ready, willing, and able to perform instant surgery on the hand of any person rash enough to attempt to pet him. Thus he sat in well-respected privacy on his open perch in the living room. One day a friend of the owner stopped by with his three-year-old daughter, and in the initial exchange of greetings the child was forgotten. When the adults finally looked around for her they were horrified to see that she was almost literally mopping up the floor with the parrot, who was enduring this indignity with a resigned expression as if to say, "Well, what can you expect from one so young?" Perhaps this empathy between youth and the lower animals was best set forth by the poet Wordsworth in his "Ode on Intimations of Immortality," wherein he states: "Heaven lies about us in our infancy." It is during this time, perhaps, that every person enjoys a kinship with Nature free from the concept of dominance or superiority that eventually tarnishes and destroys the relationship.

But since no one can remain forever young and not everyone possesses "instant appeal" for birds, what chance has the average person of getting a bird to talk? Fortunately, the trainer and his qualifications, or lack of them, are only half of the "talking bird" equation. The other half is the bird, and here individuals vary in what they demand from a trainer. My first talking budgie, Frisky, was very selective and, faced with a choice between my mother and me, chose her as his exclusive trainer. On the other hand, Frosty, my next parakeet, was an extrovert who would imitate anyone. Most birds probably fall between these two extremes. Also, individuals of the same species vary in their aptitude for mimicking and hence talking. An exception may be the greater Indian hill mynah, which, as a species, during its early years seems to have almost a compulsion for mimicking. But it is these "unknowns" in the talking bird-trainer equation that provide the challenges and hence the interest. Regardless of the type of bird you have, you will achieve some results if you make it a part of the family circle, give it exposure to your voice and personality as often as you can, and do not give up if it does not immediately return your affection. A friend who operates a kennel supply shop has a female African gray parrot which is a delight to behold. "She gets better every day," he told me as he tossed her up and down, to her evident enjoyment. It was not always so. He purchased her when she was about two years old, her clipped wing feathers giving evidence of the unsuccessful efforts by her previous owners to tame her. When she escaped from her cage one day and headed afoot for the front door and the street, the owner rushed to pick her up without first putting on gloves, whereupon she sank the tip of her beak almost through the web of his thumb. For eight months he spent time by her cage in his shop each day, extending the back of his closed fist, never his open hand, in her direction, only to have her retreat back in her cage and

If you must care for a young or injured wild bird, you must pay careful attention to the bird's dietary needs. Wood thrushes (left) and blackbirds (below) are altricial insectivores.

Meadowlarks (right) and robins (below) are altricial insectivores. In captivity they can be maintained on fruit and soft cat and/or dog food.

"growl"—a sound which conveys the same message from an African gray as from a dog. Finally, one day she moved towards him instead of away and, he said, "That was it. I have been able to do anything I want with her ever since." When a bird reacts positively instead of negatively to its owner, he may assume that he will soon hear it practicing on what he has been saying to it.

Erratic, nervous movements should be avoided while in the presence of a bird. Birds are very sensitive to any evidence of nerves on the part of their owners; indeed, veterinarians have observed that nervous owners tend to have nervous pets of any kind. On separate occasions I have had two young magpies that were reasonably tame when I got them but later became uncontrollably wild, and I am convinced this change in personality resulted from my frenzied entrances and exits as I rushed to meet the countdown for my riding pool.

Does the sex of either the bird or the trainer play any part in the training effort? Among the budgies and cockatiels the males are the superior performers; it would appear that with most of the other common talking species the sexes perform equally well. So far as sex of the trainer is concerned, it is believed that birds pick up more readily the higher pitched voices of women. However, when it comes to the personal preferences of birds as to sex of their trainers, the large parrots with which I am acquainted, at least, never seem to have heard of equal status for women. Mrs. Curtis's parrots, for instance, keep not only me at a distance but also the wives of all couples that visit them, at the same time welcoming the attention of the husbands.

Does timbre of voice play any part in teaching a bird to talk? Doubtless, as indicated above, it does play a role, but the bird's individual preference determines whom it imitates. I was told of a woman who, with her adult daughter, was a frequent guest in the home of a family that owned a parrot which was partial to the visiting mother. The voices of mother and daughter were much alike. One day the daughter alone called at the house. Hearing her voice from the adjoining room, the parrot got off his perch in the kitchen and, uttering the assorted jargon with which he greeted favored visitors, came toddling into the parlor. But when he reached the threshold and saw that the visitor was the daughter and not the mother, he instantly fell silent and, executing an aboutface, stalked scornfully out of the room. I can appreciate that daughter's discomfiture; it is not pleasant to get the cold shoulder, even from a bird.

What about loudness of voice? Parrots and mynahs are famous for their propensity for picking up swear words and ejaculations, which are normally spoken with many decibels. My aunt related an instance from her early married life when she lived on a small acreage where the nearest neighbors were a middle-aged husband and wife. The neighbors' income, derived mostly from their small truck-

Orioles, in addition to their usual insectivorous fare, enjoy fruit nectars. Baltimore orioles (left) are native American birds while yellow orioles (below) originate in South America.

Tanagers are similar to orioles in their need for soft foods and in their fondness for fruit nectar. Scarlet tanagers (right) are North American birds and blue-shouldered tanagers (below) are native to South America.

gardening operations, was less than adquate for providing the amenities of life. Nevertheless, one day the husband came home with a green parrot he had purchased for five dollars. His wife was less than enthusiastic at this acquisition, since in those days the five dollars would have bought a substantial amount of groceries. (She might have been more impressed by her husband's bargain could she have foreseen the price that her great-grandchildren would have to pay for such a bird.) The couple was noted for spirited quarrels, which usually concluded with a loud exhortation from the husband to "Shut up!" One day the wife related to my aunt that during their most recent disagreement the parrot had suddenly fixed her husband with a cold eye and exclaimed, "Shut up!" The husband was so startled by this command that he complied. These were the only words the parrot ever spoke, but he continued to say them on the appropriate occasions, and the wife confided to my aunt that for this achievement alone the parrot was worth the five dollars he had cost.

What part does repetition play in the learning process? While repetition is usually necessary in teaching a bird a phrase which is to become part of his long-term repertoire, if a casual phrase or sound appeals to him, he is quite capable of repeating it on one hearing. I know of a mynah which shouted, one time only, "Ma, where's my shirt?" A friend who owns a female African gray parrot told me that one evening his wife dropped a dish, which splintered with a crash in the sink. A few minutes later he heard the same sound again and was startled that his wife should be so careless a second time. It turned out to be the parrot repeating this complicated sound which it had heard but once. However, a bird's imitation of these casual noises may be a one-time performance, in contrast with more carefully rehearsed vocabulary. As people have learned to their embarrassment, some of these repetitious phrases may not have been intended to be immortalized in their pets' memories. Mrs. Curtis reported that a Roman Catholic family purchased one of her parakeets, but later the mother complained they were making no headway in teaching him to talk. "He's sure stupid, and we tell him so," she told Mrs. Curtis during a visit to the pet shop. "Don't be surprised," Mrs. Curtis advised, "if someday he says that." Not long after, the mother phoned Mrs. Curtis, almost in tears. She said that the parish priest had visited the family that day, and in the initial exchange of pleasantries he had walked over to the parakeet's cage, only to be greeted with "You're sure stupid." The priest's cordiality cooled considerably, and his visit did not extend to its usual length. "I know he thinks we say that about him," wailed the mother. "What can we do?" "Tell him to come by my shop," said Mrs. Curtis. "I'll tell him what you said the other day and that I told you what would happen."

Repetition implies a lapse of time, hence the question: "How long must a person repeat a phrase before the bird learns it?" This depends, of course, on the aptitude of the

Eastern bluebirds (above) and common flickers (below) both enjoy insects.

Common or winter wrens normally feed on small live foods and fruits.

bird. Deciding to "time" Frosty on a difficult phrase, before I left for work one Tuesday morning I began saying to him "Hexadecanol stops evaporation"—some of the engineering terminology I was typing at the time. By the following Saturday morning Frosty was saying this phrase so clearly that I recorded it. I was, of course, home only briefly mornings and evenings, so his lessons had been few and far between.

Words with outstanding consonants or striking syllables attract more attention and may be easier for a bird to enunciate than bland sounds. Frosty's pronunciation of the word "Minnesota" was more distinct than his rendition of the name of that state's official bird, the loon. When I decided to teach another budgie, Sugarplum, the sentence "Pieplant Cowcamp lies near Tincup," gleaned from a water resources report I had typed, the parakeet readily learned "Pieplant, Cowcamp," and "Tincup," but jumbled the "lies near." When I switched to "Pieplant Cowcamp stops at Tincup" he was soon giving an excellent account of the complete sentence. I would, therefore, suggest that the bird trainer "think big" and not make his pupil's lessons too easy.

Birds that are good at imitation have an affinity for sounds. When I was teaching Frosty the names of all the states, one evening I was repeating the name of a state which he had already learned. Piqued by his attitude of boredom, I abruptly switched to a new state, "Connecticut." As suddenly as if I had pushed a button which ejected him from his perch, he bounced off the swing and on to my side of the cage, turning his head nearly upside down in his effort to see the source of the unfamiliar sound.

Always speak slowly and enunciate clearly, and do not slight any syllables. Likewise, when whistling a tune, take a deep breath and emphasize each note. A bird "gives" what he "gets." "Missouri," for instance, in Frosty's imitation came out very much like "misery," and when I listened to my own pronunciation on the tape recorder I had to admit that his imitation was faithful to its original.

Do birds learn from each other and, if so, how about keeping two birds together? Most certainly, birds can pick up human speech "second hand." Indeed, as in the case of Sammy Steller the jay, some birds may learn only from another bird. In this regard, my studies have led me to wonder if birds possess something like ESP or mental telepathy whereby they sense when other birds, especially their own kind, are present even if they cannot see them. Audubon and Snowball were in separate rooms and never saw each other, yet Audubon repeated much of Snowball's repertoire. He also developed, on his own, a "conditioned" response, exclaiming, "Why, hello, how are you?" when Snowball, from his quarters in the front room, said, "Hello Snowball." I kept a young female magpie temporarily on my screened-in back porch. After a brief exposure to Mr. America's "Don't split my tongue," audible from his station below her in the garage, the magpie soon began to utter a slurred version of the sentence, even though she could not possibly see the speaker. These were the only words she ever learned. A male starling in my spare bedroom at the back of the house, after two years' exposure to Mortimer's "Henry" from the front room, began to repeat the word in precisely the same tone, although at that distance and through the intervening doors Mortimer's voice must have sounded very faint. Another starling on my screened-in back porch, when about six months old, began to sing like a western meadowlark, although there had not been a "real" meadowlark in my subdivision for thirty years. He undoubtedly picked up the song from his wild brethren which occasionally perched on the powerline in the alley. Admittedly he could no doubt see them, albeit from a distance, and he instinctively recognized them as his kindred.

But while such instances prove that birds do learn from

Starlings mainly feed on fruit and insects, but those living near man could be considered omnivorous.

OPPOSITE:
North American blue jays (above) and
Eurasian jays (below) are omnivorous.

each other, I would never put two untrained birds of the same species together. They would almost certainly be too interested in each other to pay any attention to human voices. Also, while an untrained bird might pick up some of the sayings of a trained neighbor, there would not be much satisfaction to the owner in having two birds of high talking potential saying the same thing. It is the birds of limited or uncertain talking ability, who otherwise might never learn anything, who stand to edify their owners most by being placed in hearing distance of more accomplished talkers.

I do not handle or touch any bird I am teaching to talk. Few birds enjoy being handled, and to force any unwelcome attention on a prospective student is likely to destroy the rapport which must exist between trainer and bird for satisfying results. Also, except for Edgar, I have kept my talking birds caged at all times. Just as teenagers' scholastic achievements often suffer if a car and other outside diversions are available, I believe birds are likely to take more interest in their lessons if their attention is not distracted with too much activity. It is said that mynahs and parrots rarely imitate in the wild, the inactivity imposed by the cage apparently being what focuses their attention on the voices of their owners.

Do birds understand the meaning of the words they say? Birds certainly can be taught to make a given response on cue, and they also may learn to do this on their own. Dr. Konrad Lorenz, the famous Austrian scientist, reported a parrot that would say "Auf Weidersehen" to a departing guest; however, the bird could not be tricked into saying these words by a "faked" exit. However, to say that a word conveys to a bird the same meaning that it does to a human being is to assume that a bird's mind is functioning at the same level as man's. Rather than trying to project my own thoughts into the consciousness of my birds, I find it more interesting to reflect on the fact that through their imitations my birds open up to me the only area in which I can

182

know for a certainty what their sensations are. When a bird whistles a tune so accurately that a person recognizes it or a raven exclaims "You're a bad boy" in a voice that a neighbor mistakes for that of its owner, the bird has proclaimed, in effect, that the sound registered on his ears in the same way as it registered on my ears. This evidence of common ground on which our levels of consciousness meet gives me a sense of fellowship with the rest of creation. This is more comfortable to me than the attitude of royal aloofness with which man isolates himself from the lower animals.

Finally, which bird should you get? That depends on (1) what you expect from the bird and (2) the size of your bank account. If you want a bird with the best speaking voice and your pocketbook can afford it, get a mynah or one of the large parrots. If you want a bird that costs nothing, is abundantly available all over the country in the spring and summer, will thrive on an inexpensive diet, can speak a number of words in a "mini-voice," and, above all, possesses in abundance that attribute which is most desirable in any pet—personality—consider the starling. Whatever its drawbacks en masse, a single starling is one of the most engaging of all pet birds, and millions of starlings could well be taken out of circulation in the wild and given an opportunity to display their more desirable characteristics as pets.

If you want a bird that is inexpensive, colorful, easy to care for, and affectionate, you could not do better than to purchase the Australian grass parakeet or budgie. This bird also, in my estimation, is the most rewarding talker. A budgie that has an aptitude for imitation will say anything its owner sets out to teach it, providing the sentences are not too long. No other "talker" to my knowledge is so reliable. No one can predict what a mynah or a parrot, for instance, will pick up. He may ignore some phrase his owner wishes to teach him and come up with a wholly unexpected item from some other source. It is true that the budgie's voice is "small" and possibly may lie beyond the range of

Finches are seed-eating
birds which thrive better in
captivity if they are also
given some animal protein.
Masked finches (left) and
Gouldian finches (below) are
often kept as caged birds by
aviculturists.

The northern blue grosbeak of North and Central America feeds on both animal and vegetable matter.

some human ears; I have read statements by obviously knowledgeable people that the budgie does not truly "talk." As a check to see if Frosty's voice is clear to anyone besides me, at my bird programs I play tape recordings of his recitation of the Peter Piper jingle without giving my audiences any clue as to what is on the tape. I find there are always some sharp-eared people present who can identify enough of the words to clue everybody in, followed by exclamations of delight from the rest of the audience as they get the complete picture.

Economics plays a part in selecting a talking pet, and many people who have their hearts set on owning a more exotic bird than the budgie and cockatiel find their plans stymied by the escalation in prices for the mynahs and large parrots, a result of the Newcastle disease quarantine in the United States. Therefore, many of these people may start thinking in terms of what the native species offer. In the United States these are found mainly among the Corvidae: the crows, ravens, magpies, and jays. Here two considerations are paramount, one of which is legal, the other moral. As to the first, a license issued by the U.S. Fish and Wildlife Service is required to keep legally any wild bird species in captivity in the United States except the starling and house sparrow. Many states also require a similar license, and prospective owners should check on these regulations with the wildlife departments of their respective states.

The second issue, which should be equally binding, is the owner's moral responsibility for the welfare of a bird that has been taken from its natural habitat and made dependent on man for board and room. Most people who go to the outlay of purchasing a parrot or a mynah do so with the intention of keeping it for life. In contrast, the person who takes, or permits his children to take, a magpie or a crow from its nest usually makes a mental reservation that if the family get tired of the bird they can simply turn it loose. Unfor-

If you want a bird you can hold, get a duck or a pigeon.

A raven is *not* a cuddly pet.

MY NOMINATIONS:

Best "human" voice: Indian hill mynah.

Best vocabulary: budgie.

Best whistler: cockatiel.

189

Least expensive (free):
starling (left).

Most expensive:
cockatoo (below left)
or macaw (below right).

Most intelligent: raven.

tunately, even the more intelligent species have difficulty fending for themselves if thrown out on their own resources after having been held in captivity. The conscientious pet owner will honor his unwritten contract with Nature and keep the bird, even a starling, to the end of its days. But the lifespans of many of the large species in captivity can be dismayingly long. One of the ravens at the Tower of London lived there for forty-four years. I was told of a magpie, kept in only semi-captivity, that disappeared after sixteen years. I now have several magpies, jays, and starlings which have outlived their usefulness to me by as much as ten years but who still occupy space on my premises. Their daily maintenance has become burdensome but is an obligation I assumed when I first welcomed them to my project.

Before a person commits himself to obtaining a large bird he should consider the fact that such a bird requires a large cage and thus takes up more space than a smaller species. I have had much better success in getting a response from my birds by "living in" with them, and I can attest to the fact that keeping a large bird indoors presents a major housekeeping problem.

So, to return to the question, what bird should you get? Only the person involved can answer that for himself. But from the lowly starling to the elegant macaw and the majestic raven, Nature's bounty has provided candidates that can fulfill every human expectation and among which each person can find his own "dream bird."

No one has yet proven "for the record" whether or not a paradise whydah can talk.

CHAPTER XVI

Would You Repeat That for the Record?

"A picture is worth 10,000 words" is a familiar maxim. But it was not until I was deeply involved in both tape recordings and talking birds that I realized only a word or two on a disk or tape may likewise be worth 10,000 words. This paradox occurs, of course, when the few words are spoken by a bird into a microphone and the 10,000 words are spoken by a mere human being.

Pet owners and doting grandmas share one thing in common: both are anxious to show off the talents of the objects of their affections. The grandmas have the advantage over the pet owners: grandchildren can usually be heard as well as seen. The pet owners, on the other hand, can never predict how their proteges will perform. This is especially true of talking birds. It is at the very time when the proud owner is anxious to display his bird's linguistic accomplishments, on a TV show for instance, that the pet chooses to remain silent. The literature on cage birds is full of accounts of the remarkable performances of individual parrots and mynahs which whistled tunes, sang operatic arias, and recited whole paragraphs of the Declaration of Independence. Alas, these glowing accounts are open to challenge simply because proof of such virtuosity via a recording is lacking. In this electronic age when tape decks are as easy to obtain as hi-fi equipment, the person who has a bird with an outstanding repertoire should make the effort to obtain proof of his pet's ability by making a recording of the performance.

And effort it may take indeed. In my case, of course, it was essential to get a permanent record of each bird's vocal achievements in order to illustrate its voice. When Frosty the parakeet proved his versatility as a linguist, I had the happy thought that it would be appropriate if I had him "introduce"—via tape—the various bird songs as I presented them at programs. I soon discovered that recording him was a project second only to getting him to say the names of the birds in the first place. My hat is off to those dedicated individuals who record birds in the wild. In addition to having their equipment running at the time the subject vocalizes, they have to second-guess where the bird will be when he "sounds off." At least in my case the bird was confined to one spot, and I could set up my equipment with the certainty that when he did talk he would be within range of the microphone. In recording out-of-doors there is interference from numerous sources—the weather and extraneous man-made and natural noises. I found, however, that there are more noises in the human household, on the street, and in the air than I had ever dreamed. One never-to-be-forgotten summer I recorded the complete gamut of sounds made by a neighbor boy's pride and joy—a motor bike. If the number of dogs and frequency of their barking as indicated on my recordings are any criterion for safety of a neighborhood from break-ins or vandalism, our community is virtually burglar-proof. And while the Air Age, in general, has been a boon to mankind, it has frustrated nature recorders on every continent except, perhaps, the Antarctic. While the drone of an airplane in the background would not be amiss in any 20th Century production, it seemed quite out of context in a setting by Shakespeare or during Poe's somber brooding on a midnight dreary in the 1840's.

But as if complications arising from the outside were not enough, the birds themselves created numerous problems. In justice to them it may be said that, unlike many people,

Parakeets can be expecially vocal, but their vocalizations often include an assortment of sounds—not all of them human.

they know better than to talk all the time. Thus there are long periods when they do not utter a sound—usually when the tape recorder is turned on! By trial and error I learned that around 9 a.m., noon, and 3 p.m. they were likely to make some conversation; therefore, I would turn on my tape recorder at those hours and often find that, like the motion picture photographer whose film runs out just as the best action is developing, my tape ran off the reel just when the birds were waxing most vocal. I also found that just because a bird *can* talk plainly, there is no assurance that he *will* talk plainly. Parakeets in particular, once they have become bilingual, enjoy mixing their natural jargon with their human vocabulary. Thus, I filled up tape after tape with Frosty's chatter, often having only three or four phrases or even words on a whole tape that did justice to his abilities.

But if getting an ideal recording of a parakeet's repertoire is difficult, parakeets themselves are particularly poor inmates to have around when one is trying to record another bird. When Peter Pan the cockatiel had progressed well along with whistling "Let's All Sing Like the Birdies Sing," I set up my tape recorder to document each segment. I soon found there was a running commentary from the parakeets in the background on virtually every "take" I made. When I took the parakeets out of the room, as well as Greenjeans the canary-winged parakeet whose raucous screech was synchronized with every worthwhile solo by Peter Pan, the cockatiel favored me with one of his least-productive recording sessions. Birds stimulate each other to perform, and usually when some stop, all stop. I eventually decided that my future audiences would have to regard the background chirping as an orchestral accompaniment to the soloist.

I also found that, as often happens in any effort, the projects I had expected to be hard were actually easy to achieve, while those with which I had anticipated no problems were beset with obstacles. I had thought that securing a raven's "Nevermore" on record would represent the ultimate in my achievements with talking birds and, consequently, would be the most difficult to attain. But getting Edgar to say "Nevermore" and then recording the word turned out to be child's play compared to the roadblocks I encountered attempting to get on tape a satisfactory "Mortimer" from the starling. He never did say the word loud enough to be very impressive, and getting a recognizable statement of it on record occupied my spare time off and on for several years. Noting that the starling occasionally gave a squeaky "Mortimer" apparently as an exclamation to take note of my comings and goings through the front door, I would turn on the tape recorder and then stage elaborate exits and entrances. The vibrations transmitted up through the base of the microphone stand to the mike itself made my

196

footsteps sound like an elephant stomping through the jungle. I eventually had to settle for a few faint "Mortimer's," comparatively free from extraneous noises, which I used for my sequence of Hotspur's imagined confrontation between a starling and Henry IV.

I found, too, that my birds had other characteristics besides temperament which interfered with their recording sessions. Birds apparently talk when there is nothing else for entertainment, and when there are human activities to watch they become an interested but silent audience. Friends who were mystified that any woman could have so little to show in the way of housekeeping as I had for a three-day week-end would have been exasperated to have found me whiling away those golden hours lying abed, reading, or, at best, sewing on buttons. Yet I know of few other activities in which a person can engage, however clandestinely, that John Q. Magpie, supersleuth, cannot detect and infer—correctly, of course—that his owner is holding out on him. Early in Edgar's career, when I was particularly excited about getting his first words on record, he was having enough of a gabfest one day that I turned on my tape recorder. I then quietly seated myself at the front-room table to "monitor" his program. However, there was immediately a cessation of sound from his room. Glancing towards the door into the hallway, which was in line with the bedroom door, I saw that Edgar had stationed himself at the outermost edge of his cage where, of course, he could get as much of a view of me as I could of him. Hastily closing the hall door, thus shutting out my distracting image, I resumed my vigil at the front-room table and was presently rewarded by a resumption of his vocal efforts.

Microphone sensitivity is another reason why a person cannot engage in any audible activities with a tape recorder running. Even "mild" movements such as sorting out papers can sound like a forest fire on tape. The best way a person can put in his time during a recording session is to

The end product—all this work for one little tape!

monitor the bird's performance, thus eliminating the need to rerun the tape later to determine if anything is on it that is worth keeping. Figeting in a dark hallway, hoping that a bird will say the desired phrase when the recorder is operating, is no time to contemplate the ancient theory that "man shall have dominion over all." At such a time the bird is in the "driver's seat," and nothing that man can do will inspire that bird brain to program any desired sound. Just as a "watched pot never boils," a listened-to bird does not talk, and one must acknowledge that there are times when a bird's mind takes precedence over man's.

But in spite of all the frustrations, the law of averages dictates that anyone who persists with his recording efforts long enough must meet with some measure of success, and I finally acquired some bird dialogue. I then set about the much easier task of rounding up recordings of the Ham clan and other human speakers to incorporate in my finished product. By using two tape recorders, of course, it is possible to put together an exchange of conversation between birds and man. Hearing Frosty recite the list of states and state birds, or Edgar filling in after the famous "Quoth the raven," my audiences have often asked how did I get the birds to say the right thing at the right time. My answer has to be, "I didn't—it was all done, not with mirrors, but with tape recorders."

So, speaking from long experience, I can assure anyone who documents his bird's speaking achievements that the effort is worth it. Even if a person does not have a project so ambitious as mine in view, such evidence frees the pet owner from the predicament of the fisherman who all too often comes home only with a description of "the one that got away." The owner who can substantiate his claims by simply flipping a switch in case his pet proves recalcitrant is freed from the embarrassment of having to tell a skeptical audience, "It's funny he is so quiet today; yesterday he was talking up a storm!"

All birds kept in captivity, whether wild, like these red-winged blackbirds, or tame, must be cared for properly.

CHAPTER XVII

Keeping Them Healthy

An acquaintance with whom I was discussing my favorite topic, talking birds, recalled from her youth a crow, evidently escaped or released from captivity, which visited their farm house each day, tapped at the window, and uttered the one word in its vocabulary: "Food." Could he have included also the phrase "Baby, it's cold in here" and "Send in the Cleanup Squad," his conversation would have covered the ABC's of cagebird care. Its diet, the "climate" of the room in which it is located, and the conditions of sanitation with which it is surrounded determine to a large extent the well-being and lifespan of any caged bird.

Every establishment that sells birds also stocks a number of publications which contain information on the proper care of the common cage birds. Anyone buying a bird should also purchase a copy of a booklet covering the species to which his bird belongs and follow the advice given therein. Much distress to both bird and owner would be avoided by so doing. To such advice I would only add an emphasis on the importance of avoiding the most common source of bird ailments: uneven temperatures and drafts. I have been the recipient of many parakeets with respiratory infections whose owners were anxious to be freed of the painful experience of watching their pets' decline. Many people have the notion that to be happy and healthy their birds should have sunshine and be able to look outdoors. However, the canary with the "view" is likely to be short-lived compared to the bird that does not enjoy these amenities. On a windy day cold air can seep in around even a "tight" window. A good diet, supplemented with vitamin drops, will make up for any lack of sunshine, and human companionship and attention will relieve any boredom a bird may feel behind closed drapes or in a dark but cozy corner of a room.

Many people also feel it is wrong to keep a bird caged at all times. Here again, the "liberated" parakeet is not likely to set any record for longevity. There is, of course, much satisfaction in being greeted with a swoop onto one's shoulder and a welcoming chirp from a parakeet who is free to explore his surroundings. To offset this advantage there is the sleepless night after a bird has flown out a window "that is never opened," been caught by the cat or dog that is "never allowed in the house," or has ridden, unnoticed, out-of-doors on the shoulder of his owner and flown off into the cold night. Many birds have been killed by a door slamming on them, and I heard of one freak accident when a member of the family tripped over a doorsill and fell flat on the floor at the spot where the parakeet was sitting. In spite of all my precautions, Picklepuss had one narrow escape when I had let him out of his cage to have a little exercise on top of a cupboard and failed to notice he had flown down on the floor and was following me around. Stepping

"Don't tread on me"

back from replenishing his seed cup, I inadvertently kicked him—fortunately—rather than stepping on him. No one molests a cockatoo, even unintentionally, and comes off unscathed. He latched onto my leg like a "jumping" cactus, squealing and biting furiously. I was so thankful he was in any condition to retaliate that I endured his chastisement meekly until I could hobble over to a table where I kept a heavy corduroy cloth. Here I succeeded in transferring his wrath from my leg to the cloth, after which I contemplated the damage to my leg, which, fortunately, was not so irreparable as the damage to my new stocking.

There are, of course, other pitfalls which may menace a bird, not all of which can be anticipated by any owner. Birds are extremely high-strung and may have heart attacks brought on by shock. Mrs. Curtis reported a bizarre incident when one of her customers left a canary with a friend who lived on a lower floor in the same apartment house. Upon her return the owner phoned her friend, who decided to bring the canary up to her. But as the neighbor started up the stairs with the cage, the bird gave a sharp chirp and dropped dead. In going over the incident, the two women arrived at a conclusion with which their veterinarian concurred. At the top of the stairs hung a mounted moose head, the glass eyes of which may have cast a reflection that added to the already fearsome aspect presented to the bird as he was borne closer to it. Fatal shock resulted. For the good of his pet, the owner should attempt to keep it in familiar surroundings and, if possible, in the same cage.

The larger "wild" birds, such as the magpie, crow, and raven, while they also panic easily, are more hardy and can survive startling incidents as well as more extreme temperatures. They are also "omnivorous" and therefore are not so specialized as to dietary requirements. It is quite true that these birds will eat almost anything. This does not mean, however, that they should be fed "anything." The most satisfactory basic diet I have found for these birds is

In the wild the diet of a red-shafted flicker, common in western North America, consists mainly of insects.

dogfood, both the soaked pellets and the canned. However, like humans, my birds have indicated that they enjoy some variety. Henry the crow was particularly human in his response to the same old fare, often uttering a grumpy "um-um-um" as he inspected what he evidently regarded as the unappetizing menu spread before him. I occasionally offered to these large birds a variety of items which, although not conventional bird fare, could do no harm—bits of processed cheese, unsalted crackers, graham crackers, grapes, raisins, apples. Peanut butter spread on the crackers was a special treat, Edgar often daintily nipping off the glob of peanut butter before he went on to take the whole cracker from my fingers. All of the Corvidae liked dried bread, which they soaked in their water dishes until the dough reached the desired consistency. Pancakes, muffins, cornbread, and plain doughnuts were eagerly accepted, although I gave the doughnuts but sparingly. Too much fat or grease is a "no-no" in the diet of a bird kept in the inactive status of a house pet. Chunks of unsalted dry cottage cheese were appreciated only by Miss America the magpie. Meat, either fresh or cooked, was, of course, highly regarded by all, but at the prices it ultimately reached I had to take it off their menu except for the lower priced items such as liver, heart, and kidney. Hard-boiled egg was the most enthusiastically received of all my offerings, and it is not hard to understand why wild birds regard these egg epicures as their special enemies.

Curiously enough, Henry—whose species is synonymous with cornfield raiders—was not impressed by corn in any form—canned, dried, raw, cooked, or on the cob. Items that I never offered were candy, frostings, glazed fruits, or any kind of "gooey" stuff, such as candied popcorn. Sweet potatoes, I learned, did not agree with Edgar. The magpies liked nightcrawlers, and their curiosity impelled them to investigate caterpillars and tomato worms. However, while crows in the wild devour large amounts of such natural food, my Henry's instinctive suspicion of anything un-familiar led him to behave as if he would not touch those creepy things with a ten-foot pole.

All of my bluejays have favored soaked dogmeal, plenty of unsalted soda crackers, shelled peanuts, and sunflower seeds. Mortimer Starling the First has refused to eat any-thing but a crumbly brand of canned dogfood always topped with mashed hard-boiled egg. The rest of my starl-ings have lived entirely on soaked dogmeal, with live mealworms as a special treat.

I never attempted to keep gravel before my house guests except for the parrot-types and finches, which are, of course, primarily seed-eaters and must have gravel to grind their food. Mynahs, with their specialized diets of mynah meal or pellets, plus some fruit, do not need gravel. The crows, ravens, magpies, and jays might have benefited from the oystershell and other mineral supplements contained in the processed bird grits on the market. However, it would have taken more ingenuity than I possessed to have wired

J.C. RIGLI-76

"If the chow doesn't improve, I'm going "over the hill."

some sort of removable container on the dog-cages in which I kept these birds, which they could not have wrenched loose, scattering the contents on the floor. Although plagued with a variety of alien substances on my floors and carpets, I did not wish to convert them to sandpaper, particularly since the birds remained healthy without such roughage in their diets.

That a caged bird must depend on his owner to "vacuum" his cage and wash his dishes is obvious, but it is rather startling to find how many people do not change the papers in their birds' cages regularly or wash the seed and water cups, scrape the perches, and check for mites and other bird parasites. The cages of mynahs especially stand in need of daily attention; it is said that pellets or moist mynah meal pass through the bird's system in about eighteen minutes. A friend to whom I imparted this bit of avian lore jovially suggested that the solution to the problem lay in putting the bird outdoors every eighteen minutes! This being rather impractical, the owner of one of these valuable birds should keep it in a cage equipped with a grate through which the copious droppings may fall, and clean the grate and change the papers at least once a day. Mynahs also like to sleep on the floor of their cages, sheltered by a paper bag or a section of the daily paper with several pages folded over to make a "bedroll."

Paper is the most easily disposed of carpeting for the cage of any bird, and newspaper, of course, is the most readily available and least expensive. Almost all birds like to chew on or tear paper, and the magpies, apparently to amuse themselves, will "chink up" various crannies in their cages with paper which they have soaked in their water dishes. The resulting decorative effects are startling, to say the least. Edgar ripped paper endlessly, scattering the pieces far outside his cage or dropping them into a space between two half-opened windows. This preoccupation with newspaper has never harmed any of the birds in whose cages I

"Hey, I can't sleep lying down!"

have kept newspaper; however, there have been cases of lead poisoning reported which were attributed to the lead in the newsprint being absorbed by cage birds chewing on the paper or soaking it in their drinking water. For that reason I have never kept newspaper in Picklepuss's cage or in the cage of other especially valued small birds I have owned.

Ownership of a bird or any other pet imposes extra work. Solomon perhaps stated it best in his proverbs when he wrote, "Where no oxen are, the crib is clean." Then he added astutely, "But much increase is in the strength of oxen." A pet may well provide its owner with that extra element of strength for the day which makes the additional effort worthwhile.

People who keep birds also should be aware of the fact that "outside birds," whether wild species or escaped cage birds involved in a rescue effort, could carry infectious diseases and should be kept separate from any valuable pets

"This is more like it."

"Is it morning so soon?"

until their state of health is determined. In this connection, I have been reminded by some of my health-conscious friends that I might be endangering my own health also by my close association with birds. My attitude in this regard is that, since there is no absolute security in this world for either man or beast, every person must determine what elements constitute "quality of life" for himself and, after taking reasonable precautions, proceed on his quest with confidence. For myself, "quality of life" includes association with birds, and the mental uplift I receive from them more than offsets any conceivable risks I may encounter in the company of my feathered friends.

But just as human beings vary in their resistance to disease and in longevity, birds are subject to a number of disorders beyond the control of even a conscientious owner. Parakeets and canaries are subject to heart attacks as they grow older. Budgies frequently develop tumors in almost any part of their anatomy. Because of the possibility of egg-binding and other disorders associated with reproduction, females are often less long-lived than the males, although the oldest budgie I ever saw—sixteen years of age—was a female.

Yes, our pets who share our homes and our lives are subject to the same infirmities of the flesh as we are. I go occasionally to a local pet cemetery with Mrs. Curtis where several of her pets are buried. Looking at the little headstones, I find much that tells of the characters of both pets and owners, as well as the relationships that existed between them. The epitaph "Our darling Fluffy" was probably selected by a woman, and the photograph embedded in the stone shows that the name was descriptive of the cat. "Bestest little dog in the world" could have been a tribute from either a man or a woman. But a lengthy inscription on a large headstone was almost certainly composed by a man: "Dear Red, my fondest hope is that we will meet some day and hunt together again."

But dogs and cats are not the only pets that occupy such a niche in the hearts of their owners that they merit a monument in their memory. In the shade of an elm near the spot where two of Mrs. Curtis's parrots are buried is a smooth gray stone with a beautifully etched likeness of a cockatiel and the inscription: "To Cockie, our pet cockatiel, aged eight years," which attests to the role which birds can play in the lives of their owners. As wild birds and animals become fewer, man's attention will inevitably focus more and more on human beings and human activities, and his pets will become increasingly his only contact with Nature and the nonhuman world. Then the role of pets will become even more important in providing those outside contacts which man must have in order to develop his full capacity as a human being. Thus it will behoove him to understand and comply with the requirements fixed by Nature for the welfare of his pets, as he comes to realize that, in a sense, his own well-being is bound up with theirs.

Many people consider pigeons to be pests, but these "pests" could easily become favorite pets.

CHAPTER XVIII

The Trouble with Keeping Birds Is—

One of my bosses told me that her husband would not let her keep even a parakeet or canary because he believed a bird in the house is bad luck. At the time I considered myself fortunate that I did not share this superstition; however, as I got deeper into aviculture I was forced to acknowledge that ownership of birds, whether they are inside the house or out, can present unexpected complications and disrupt the ordinary day-to-day living. Depending on circumstances, these incidents may be amusing, frustrating, or downright dangerous. Some of the problems I have encountered which remain vivid in my memory are set forth in the following pages.

Birds can create opportunities for misunderstanding. Carrying a bird cage on my way to a downtown hotel to pick up an unwanted pigeon, I passed a couple of small boys, one of whom, noticing that my cage was empty, exclaimed in consternation, "Hey, lady, you've lost your bird!" However, my activities were a puzzlement to more than small boys when I took my battery-powered tape recorder to our annual stockshow one winter morning to record some rooster crows for later imitation by my birds. I was soon running up and down the aisles in the poultry exhibits trying to single out the most consistent performers. I was somewhat taken aback, however, when I realized my own antics were attracting almost as much of an audience as the feathered exhibits. The quizzical gaze of one man in particular called for an explanation, so I attempted to enlighten him. "I have some talking birds at home and am recording some crows for them to imitate," I explained. My listener's bewilderment obviously deepened, and I elaborated further. "I have a crow at home and I thought he might imitate some rooster crows." The expression on the man's face indicated he had lost me completely, and he moved on. When my next group of spectators assembled I was more specific. "I teach birds to talk. I am writing a book on talking birds. They imitate different sounds, and I thought they might imitate some rooster crows if I could record some." A puzzled silence followed this announcement, and I expanded my presentation. "The crowing of these roosters is an interesting sound. If I play my recordings back, perhaps my pet crow will imitate them." I realized immediately I should not have mixed my "crows," but one woman's face registered comprehension. "So *that's* what they're doing!" she exclaimed. Suddenly I felt very old. My vocabulary, which had always included the words "crowing" and "crow" in connection with roosters, had become antiquated to today's city-bred generation. "Rooster crows" to my audience obviously meant "male crows." When relating the incident to friends later, I reduced my definitions to the simplest terms. "When a rooster says 'cockadoodle-do," I stated, "he is crowing, and the 'cockadoodle-do' itself is called a 'crow'—no relation to my Henry the crow, of course."

Birds can create strained and embarrassing relations with unexpected visitors. Snowball the mynah bird, from his quarters near the front door, became my official "greeter," giving a rousing "Hi!" whenever anybody came up on the porch. On one occasion when I was working in the yard of the house which I owned next door, I observed two magazine salesmen on my doorstep. From my partial concealment among the bushes I could hear them ringing the doorbell and, through the locked screen door, Snowball's response. Shading their eyes in an effort to see who was ac-

214

I wanted to see if my crow could crow (like a rooster).

knowledging their presence but not answering the doorbell, they peered through the door so long that, with Snowball's repeated encouragement, I feared they would stay all afternoon. I came out of hiding, explained that what they were hearing was a bird, and in our resulting discussion the impersonal relationship between salesman and customer was replaced by the more congenial bond among persons sharing a mutual interest. When inevitably they recalled their business and began to promote the literature they were selling, my resistance was diminished, and I subscribed to several magazines I had not intended to add to the growing stack of publications to which I already gave very superficial review.

Snowball's cordiality eventually involved him in even deeper negotiations with a visitor of quite a different sort. Mrs. Ham was taking care of the birds at my house one day when an efficient-looking gentleman with a briefcase appeared at the door. Resolving not to repeat my performance, she was prepared to tell him that she could not

Finches are small birds; if left uncaged they could easily be attacked by larger birds—or stepped on by their owner.

make purchases in the name of the owner. However, when he produced credentials identifying him as an investigator for the FBI, she listened respectfully to what he had to say. He explained that the previous day two men had held up a neighborhood bank, and the FBI was investigating all persons who had conducted business there at or near the time of the robbery. This investigation was to ascertain whether those clients had any knowledge of the appearance of the hold-up men or their vehicle. The name of the young woman living in my basement was on this list. Mrs. Ham explained that the girl was attending classes at the nearby university and offered to look up her phone number so the investigator could call her later. For this purpose the two consulted the telephone book at the front-room table, unaware that behind them Snowball was undergoing a crisis of his own. In fact, he was wrestling with the problem that plagued Hamlet: decision-making. On the one hand, his survival instinct warned him to remain inconspicuous, and therefore silent, in the presence of a stranger. On the other hand, he had an overwhelming compulsion to join in a conversation in which his favorite person, Mrs. Ham, was taking part. Finally, throwing caution to the winds, he sounded out with a full-throated "Hi!" The officer swung around. "What was that?" he demanded. "How are you?" Snowball said sociably. "It's the bird," Mrs. Ham hastened to explain. "All of these birds talk." The agent relaxed with a grin. "Well, you certainly gave me a start," he said to the impertinent little interloper. When Mrs. Ham related the incident to me that evening, we both jovially agreed that had Snowball been trained to say "Stick'em up!" there would have been one nosy little mynah who would have found himself a real jailbird in Leavenworth. "Either that," said a railroad detective to whom I related the story, "or there would have been a big pile of feathers in that corner!"

Birds can create hazards for other occupants of the household, human or otherwise. Where there are a number of birds present, occasionally a cage door inadvertently will be left unlatched, and the owner will find an empty cage, necessitating an immediate search under dressers and behind drapes for the escaped inmate. Fortunately for one of my starlings, he made such an escape at a time when I was present. He headed straight down the hall for my bedroom just when, as luck would have it, Edgar was enjoying a "liberty" break. He was perched on one of the dressers when the feathered Daniel made his fearless entrance into the lion's den. Edgar had never captured any prey larger than a moth, but he met the challenge in the best tradition of his kind, dropping instantly to the floor and setting off in hot pursuit of the scampering little varmint. The state's starling population would have been speedily reduced by one had not Edgar been so intent on the chase that he failed to notice me bearing down upon him at full speed from behind. The episode ended with both birds being thrust rather unceremoniously back into their respective cages.

On another occasion Edgar, through no fault of his own, became a hazard to my own well-being. One evening I heard the drone of the police helicopter and saw its probing searchlight pass across my house and yard. Wondering what miscreant was in the neighborhood, I locked the front door and headed for the bathroom. As I entered I just got a glimpse of Edgar perched on the bathtub before he launched himself straight for my head. I automatically ducked, but Edgar groped for a toehold. One of his feet, armed with half-inch-long toenails, slashed across my face, mercifully missing my eye but catching the bow of my glasses, sending them spinning off into space. It was not until I had time to consider the episode afterwards that I realized how Edgar happened to be in the bathroom. Always suspicious of the unfamiliar, ordinarily he never set foot even through the threshold of his bedroom door. Evidently, the beam of the helicopter searchlight had flashed across the room while he was out of his cage. His startled leap had carried him inadvertently through the bedroom door into the hall where,

completely disoriented, he made another lunge which landed him in the bathroom. Thus, when I suddenly appeared in the doorway he had sought refuge on my familiar form. Walking stooped-over, with him riding on the back of my neck, I delivered him to his room, where he immediately fled for security to his cage. Thankful that my eye had been spared but certain that my glasses—the only pair I had—were shattered on the tile floor, I groped my way back to the bathroom to retrieve at least the frames. On rare occasions something may be said on behalf of even bad habits: a terrycloth towel had fallen earlier off the towel rack onto the floor. I had carelessly let it lie there and cushioned in its soft folds I found, still intact, the missing specs!

If, instead of being a well-organized individual who goes about his business in an efficient manner, a person goes blundering from one project to another, ownership of birds widens the opportunity for unforeseen crises to occur. I decided to suspend Edgar's dog cage on lengths of pipe inserted in holes in two sawhorses. To get such pipes in the required length I drove to a metal yard one Saturday morning just after a heavy storm had deposited a foot of snow, obscuring to that depth all perceptible features on the roadway. During a previous visit to the warehouse I had driven along a high board fence. Noting such a fence on my present expedition, I turned into a "street"—failing to observe that I was a block below where I had turned previously. In so doing I missed one of the most important of all highway warning signs. It was not until my car ground to a halt with an angry snort that I realized I was not on a street at all but hung up on the mainline tracks which carried all northbound rail traffic into Denver! No amount of spinning the wheels made my vehicle self-propelling again. The car, fifteen years old, would not be a great financial loss, but what about my liability for disrupting train traffic or possible damage to a locomotive in the event a train came through? Already I thought I heard a train whistling in the distance.

I ran to the intersection, thinking I could make a phone call to some traffic control center that would warn any inbound train crew of an obstruction ahead. I was momentarily diverted by the approach of a very heavy-set man, intent—I afterwards suspected—on being the first in line when the local pub opened. When I pointed out my predicament to him, he showed consternation but not much enthusiasm for putting his considerable bulk to work trying to dislodge my car. A pickup truck with a man and woman in it paused at the railroad crossing. Frantically, I presented my appeal to them. The man took in the situation, turned the wheel over to his wife, and removed from his tool kit the most welcome human invention I could have imagined at that time, a heavy tow chain and hook. Fastening the hook to my bumper and the other end to his truck, the man shouted instructions to his wife. The truck made several heaves, then appeared to bog down itself. My head throbbed worse than before. What if the truck likewise became a casualty of my folly?

If all the trains I thought I heard whistling in the distance had actually come into Denver that morning, the railroad yards would have had their heaviest traffic since the dawn of the Jet Age. But the woman knew both her vehicle and her driving techniques. More shouted instructions and spinning of wheels and suddenly both vehicles were on solid ground beyond the rail crossing. An hour later, with my car safely in the driveway, I did hear a bona fide train whistle in the distance, and I realized this was one incident I should remember with gratitude in case, at some future time, I got into a predicament which did not have such a happy ending.

Birds can divert people's attention from their jobs. Returning home late one evening, I was aghast to find the screen pried off the window of my bedroom in the basement and a big dirty footprint on the sheet where an intruder had stepped down onto my bed. Unaccountably, a

What is the difference between a raven and a crow? "Elementary, my
dear Watson. The raven is bigger than a crow!" Both birds, however,
can be mischievous.

portable radio-tape recorder and a portable TV on a stand beside the bed had not been taken, although they could have been shoved easily through the window even if the thief had made a hasty exit. Two patrolmen promptly answered my anguished call, but when they found the theft was minor, possibly some tape cassettes whose number I could not determine accurately, they became more interested in the antics of my birds than in the footprint on my bed. Instead of playing the role of a victim of a break-in, I found myself giving a lecture on talking birds to what was without exception the most attentive audience I have ever addressed. The Hams and I agreed afterwards, however, that my birds had acquired two friends on the police force who undoubtedly would make every effort to apprehend the culprit should anyone ever disturb them.

Keeping birds may be hazardous to personal belongings. The propensity of magpies and crows for taking bright objects is legendary, and my larger pupils lived up fully to this reputation. Henry the crow improved upon it by extending his choice of objects to even lusterless ones. Reaching down into a drawer carelessly left ajar in my typewriter desk, he removed a whole sheet of whooping crane postage stamps of ancient vintage which I was saving for affixing to special letters. These he ripped up as efficiently as a paper shredder.

Suzie Q. the magpie in my bedroom, however, had considerably more opportunity to indulge in her fondness for bright objects because I had more jewelry in dresser drawers in that room. When I stepped, simultaneously, on an earring in one bedroom slipper left under my bed and a bobbypin in the other, I realized there was mischief afoot. Soon after I saw her sprinting across the floor with an earring in her beak and realized she had gotten into my jewelry chest. I began an immediate search for any other missing items, getting down on all fours to look under the dresser. With the curious sixth sense which enables the more intelligent animals to share their masters' moods, Suzie got down on the floor with me, and when I glanced to one side I found her right beside me, tail sticking straight up, chin almost touching her feet, peering under the dresser as if to join me in a mock search for the articles whose fate was known to her alone. Only the fact that I knew there must be trust on the part of the student if he is to learn from his teacher enabled me to resist the impulse to give her a swat in the tailfeathers. This self-control allowed me to retain a measure of the magpie's confidence, but my own confidence in the magpie was shattered. I removed the remaining contents of the jewelry box to safer quarters, leaving her to amuse herself with less valuable trinkets, such as bobbypins and hair clips.

Because of his greater bulk, when Edgar occupied the same room he was unable to manipulate the various containers to his own advantage. I purposefully kept them

I discovered that ravens are as interested in shiny objects as magpies and crows.

placed at angles which left insufficient room for him to operate conveniently. Hence, he made only one real "haul," which was, however, a "beaut." During one of my cleanings of the bedroom, my attention was attracted to a shiny object on the floor in a corner. Picking it up I found to my dismay that it was one of a pair of my most expensive earrings, kept in one of the heavy bureau drawers which, if it was tightly closed, he could not open. Obviously the drawer had not been completely shut on some occasion, and he had inserted his beak into the crevice and removed the most valuable of the belongings I had stored in that drawer. I searched the floor in vain for one stone which was

Blue jays, too, are capable of much mischief.

missing and then noticed that the mate to the earring was also gone. I studied the hole Edgar had pounded in the plastered wall beside his cage, obvious thoughts running through my mind. What good would it do my heirs at some future time to inherit one earring placed for security in a raven's wall safe?

During my fruitless search, Edgar had been a silent but interested spectator from his perch atop his cage, but when I finally turned my back and prepared to leave the room he pronounced his verdict against himself in profound tones: "Baad boy!" No more fitting words could have been found to express my sentiments at that time. Of course I was to blame for having left the drawer partially open in the first place, but since most of my jewelry is strictly of the bargain basement variety, why, I wondered glumly, couldn't he have taken some of that? And then I realized Edgar followed by instinct a principle which one of the most famous thieves in literature—Fagin in Charles Dickens's *Oliver Twist*—had to learn first for himself and then pass on to his young trainees in crime: "Don't steal trash; take 'only the best.'"

CHAPTER XIX

In the Footsteps of Nellie

One of the lesser known works of Louisa May Alcott, author of the famous *Little Women,* is a multi-volume set of short stories titled *Aunt Jo's Scrapbag.* Thanks to my grandmother's choice of literary gifts, I had access to a large selection of this author's output in my early years. While the more famous Alcott books, *Little Women, Little Men,* and *Jo's Boys,* received the bulk of my attention, *Aunt Jo's Scrapbag* also came under my scrutiny.

One story in particular, titled "Nellie's Hospital," caught my fancy. Nellie was the small sister of a young Civil War veteran who was recuperating at home from wounds suffered in that conflict. Her thoughts naturally being preoccupied with health and nursing problems, Nellie decided to conduct a hospital service for injured animals. Being familiar with the covered wagons which served as ambulances in that era, Nellie undertook to pick up her patients in her own toy wagon, which her brother, to pass the time, outfitted with a cover and some of the supplies carried by the full-sized vehicles. Among her first patients was a baby robin, which later became self-sufficient and flew away. This episode struck a responsive chord in my heart the summer I was reading the book, and I resolved to bring Nellie's project up to date by offering a similar service at our ranch. I had no wagon, but I fixed up a box, well padded with grass and soft cloth, and trudged around the fields and hillsides looking for likely patients. There was, however, a great scarcity of creatures needing medical attention. Possibly word had gotten around in the wildlife community that my surgical and nursing skills did not equal my

Cardinals are more famous for their beauty than their singing, though the red-crested cardinal of South America does sing well occasionally.

Virginia or red cardinals are common in North and Central America where their brilliant color makes them a stand-out against any background.

good intentions, and any animal that felt indisposed would do well to keep out of sight. A more likely explanation, however, is that, while I did not realize it, like Nellie I was living in a world still reasonably safe for man and beast. The days of superhighways, superspeed automobiles, and superinsecticides, all lethal enemies of wildlife, still lay some years in the future. Nellie's only traffic casualty was a slow-moving snake run over by a passing wagon or buggy. It never occurred to me to look alongside the dirt road that skirted our property, but it is unlikely I would have found any accident victims. There were comparatively few automobiles traversing that road in those days, and they could not have attained any high degree of speed on its numerous bumps and curves. As I recall, my only patients that summer were four mountain bluebird fledglings rescued from their nest in a hole in a fence post that had been invaded by ants. The smallest of the youngsters died, one drowned in a small pool near the house, and one unexplainably disappeared; but the fourth fledgling flew back and forth from increasing distances at our beckoning whistle. He finally followed the call of his kind, leaving me with a memory of a fragment of blue sky caught in the semblance of a bird. It is one of the pleasantest recollections of my youth.

When my carefree days on the ranch ended and, like Whittier's "Barefoot Boy," I began to "tread the mills of toil" in the city, I had little contact with birds of any kind for years, and Nellie and her hospital almost faded from memory. But that which is inborn to one's nature cannot be indefinitely stilled or forgotten. Gradually, my fondness for birds became common knowledge, and people at the office and in my neighborhood, anxious to make some humane disposition of the troublesome foundlings their children frequently discovered, began to bring their offerings to me. Like anyone else, I had no place to keep such birds except in makeshift cages and boxes in my basement. My mother wearied of never knowing when she might stumble upon an

The lark's on the wing—although this horned lark tries to mount up and regale me with song in the manner of his famous cousin the skylark, he finds his ability to soar hampered by limits imposed by the ceiling.

escapee hiding in some dark corner and finally exclaimed in exasperation, "Why don't you build a big cage outdoors for these things? You're always going to have them, a house is no place to keep them, and they aren't happy in here anyway."

I knew that a permanent solution to the problem was called for, so I spent several week-ends investigating different types of enclosures and finally agreed that my mother's proposed cage would be the most satisfactory answer. I summoned a salesman for a chain-link fence company, who came out and measured off the one-fourth of my backyard which I indicated I could devote to this purpose. He came up with a price of $300 for a six by twenty by sixteen foot cage with wire over the top and hardware cloth and chain-link fencing on the sides. This was in pre-inflation days when $300 was big money, and I threw up my hands. "Forget it," I said, "we can't afford it."

Distinguishing the sex of a bird is often quite easy—especially if you have a pair. On the left is a female yellow sparrow.

More often than not, the male bird is more colorful than the female. On the right is a male yellow sparrow.

Sparrows have thick bills which are adapted to crushing seeds; this is a black-capped sparrow.

My mother, fortunately, was not so easily discouraged. "Yes we can," she insisted. "There's no use putting up some kind of ramshackle affair that we're ashamed of and is always falling down."

I knew, of course, that she was right, so I directed the salesman to turn in the order. In a short time—perhaps because the company feared I would try to retreat from my bargain—the work crews arrived and soon had the metal fence posts in place, which made it clear to any spectators that a large enclosure was being erected on that site. A fun-loving young woman friend of mine and I were surveying the work progress one evening when a lad came down the alley and shouted, "What are you going to keep in that?" Before I could reply, my friend shot back, "PIGS." "Peegs?" the lad echoed incredulously, and he went his way, no doubt relaying this piece of information to his concerned family and neighbors. I told my smart-alec companion that if a delegation of neighbors arrived inviting me to move my proposed pigpen out of town, I would have her to blame.

No delegation arrived, but my next-door neighbor, a minister, did, courteously inquiring just what I had in mind. He had good reason for concern. The four lots on which our respective houses stood had once been owned by the same party who, with no zoning ordinances to comply with in the early days, had constructed a small house almost squarely on the line between lots two and three. Although the house had been improved considerably by succeeding owners, it still bordered my property line. The outer edge of my cage was inside my line, but it still ran uncomfortably close to the minister's dining room window. I assured him that my proposed tenants would be small in size, relatively few in number, and would occupy the premises chiefly during the summer months. The minister departed, and while he probably wondered why it was his luck to have for a neighbor a woman who took the Bible's "spar-

234

row text" so literally, he seemed satisfied with my assurances. Nevertheless, several weeks later when I arrived home from work my mother pointed to a "For Sale" sign posted on the minister's lawn. We put our heads together. One did not need ESP to recognize the potential problems posed by a bird hostelry looming next to a residence situated practically on the same property line. That evening I called on the minister, who said he had been offered a pastorate in another state. I advised him that I would like to have his property as an addition to my bird sanctuary, and he expressed satisfaction that he had to look no further for a buyer. After the inevitable wait, "closing" ceremonies were held, and my mother and I proudly assumed for ourselves the title of "Real Estate Developers." News of my coup eventually reached the office, where, all explanations to the contrary, word went round that I had used a very novel method to force the sale of property I coveted—building a chickencoop right under the nose of the owner!

Meanwhile the cage had been completed, and the fence crew was less enthusiastic, advising me that I had gotten a bargain for my $300. It was tedious work fastening the chicken wire across the top of the cage and the hardware cloth around the sides, and they could have put up one hundred feet of fence in the same time and made more money. Eventually I paid another $250 to have the cage divided into compartments so that I could keep weaker species separated from more aggressive ones, still another $350 to build a separate cage and shelter under a sunny corner of my new property, and $500 to enclose a back porch. Following in Nellie's footsteps, I found, was an expensive undertaking.

The first patients lodged in my infirmary were mourning doves, frequently winged by hunters or hit by cars. One of them, however, had been born with only a stump for its left wing. Had not one of my friends seen it take its initial plunge from the nest, it would have soon met with disaster

Doves and pigeons, such as the diamond dove (left), the turtle dove (below), and the bronze-winged pigeon (facing page), live long and healthy lives in captivity when fed with seed mixtures.

This crippled nighthawk, in threat display, has lived in captivity for two and a half years on a diet of particles of beef heart, liver, and soaked dogmeal placed in his mouth two or three times a day.

since it was, of course, quite helpless. In my cage it could live much longer than an average dove in the wild. When an egg appeared after several years, the bird's sex was unmistakably determined, and since I had another dove in the cage with an injured wing, it was evident that I had a mated pair. Each spring thereafter "Little Girl" produced about two clutches of eggs, which she and her mate took turns incubating. She determinedly marched him all over the cage if he proved reluctant to take over his shift. Apparently, along with her deformity she was also sterile, for the eggs never hatched, but I figured incubation duties gave the little couple something to do for the summer, and I never disturbed their homemaking efforts.

I later acquired a second female, permanently flightless after an encounter with an automobile, and I wondered if she would play the "femme fatale" upon introduction into my dove lovenest. However, she stayed to herself, and I concluded that a female dove does not attempt to break up an already happy union. However, as the result of a puzzling incident that occurred while these three birds were the only occupants of the cage, I was not so sure that the male can be similarly trusted.

238

I did not keep the cage locked unless it contained some bird that would be unusually attractive to someone who might stray into my yard, but one afternoon when I returned from work I found that someone obviously had been in the cage. The one-winged female was sitting on her nest; the male was likewise in attendance but missing his entire tail assembly, which I found lying in a handful in a corner of the cage. The unmated female was missing. There were no answers to the questions that immediately arose concerning the break-in. Why had the easily caught nesting female and her eggs been left unmolested? Why had the intruder not persisted in his obvious effort to catch the male? Had he taken the unattached female instead, or had she walked out the open cage door, for which she had a propensity? I locked the cage and awaited, without much hope, a "break" in the case.

I had a crawl space under my back porch, fitted with a screened gate and Plexiglas door, where I put my permanent invalids during the winter months. I had advised a few presumably trustworthy individuals that, if there was no one at the "admission office" at my house or the Hams', they could leave injured birds in that compartment. I asked that they post a note indicating they had put a bird in there, since I did not check that space regularly. The day following the mysterious happenings in the cage, however, more or less as a futile gesture I opened the door to the crawl space. There to my amazement lay the missing female, more dead than alive, her legs extended stiffly behind her, their feathers missing and the skin looking as if it had been rubbed with an abrasive. About all the relief I could offer was a little water, which she was too weak to swallow. Wishing to let her die in peace amid familiar and friendly surroundings, I raked up a pile of grass clippings in the middle of the cage, laid her on it, and left her, at least, in security. When I looked later to see how she was faring, I saw that the male dove, the time not having arrived for him

239

Gallinaceous or
ground-nesting birds
include bob whites
(left) and painted quail
(below).

240

Red junglefowl (right) and pheasants (Elliot's pheasant below) are also gallinaceous birds.

to take his shift on the eggs, had climbed up on the pile of grass and was sitting beside her, cooing intermittently. I was glad to see that he was offering her companionship in her hour of need and excused his infidelity in view of the circumstances. I wondered if his dialogue might run something like this: "Buck up, baby, you gotta get well. Life would be Dullsville in this place without you. My wife doesn't understand me. She's always bugging me to sit on those eggs. You're the one bright spot in my henpecked life. Don't leave me." Whatever the gist of his comments, she did revive. By morning she had recovered the use of her legs sufficiently to crawl off the grass heap, and in a few days she was running around as sprightly as ever. Since no neighbors ever mentioned finding and returning her, I can only assume that the bird-nappers, tiring of their prize, placed her under the porch where, had I not chanced to look soon afterwards, she would have died.

But for the most part the inmates of my cage lived undisturbed, and further generations of doves raised several young, since the cage was large enough to accommodate several large shrubs and bushes. As time passed and the availability of a bird haven became common knowledge, I found myself running a full-scale ambulance service, par-

"Don't give up the ship, Baby"!!

When is an owl not an owl?—when it's a member of the goat-sucker family, particularly the poorwill (right), western relative of the better known whippoorwill of the eastern U.S. These birds are frequently turned in to bird rescue units as "little owls."

ticularly in the summer months, during the height of the nesting season. I learned never to put my car in the garage until bedtime, since chances were I would have to take it out in response to a phone call beginning, "I've got a bird." Since many people are woefully lacking in species identification, I found it intriguing to speculate on what kind of bird awaited me when I reached my destination. I became accustomed to wrens, warblers, finches, mockingbirds, purple martins, and even crows that had been miraculously transformed into ordinary starlings by the time I arrived to claim them. I learned that a "gray bird with a small head and bill" was usually a mourning dove; nighthawks and poorwills were described as small hawks and owls; pigeons did usually remain pigeons and robins, robins. I was justified, however, in failing to identify, from the description given me over the phone, one feathered castaway. It was on a Saturday morning in August, when Denver was in the throes of an acute gasoline shortage and I could only hope that my tankful of gas would run me through the weekend, when I received a call from a resident in a town thirty miles

Ducks and ducklings have broad beaks so that they can more easily hold fish or so that they can filter seeds from the mud bottoms of ponds and lakes.

OPPOSITE:
Chicks can become quite tame, but they also can make a lot of noise—especially when they think they're lost.

away. She had found, lying in the street, a "black bird, big as a grapefruit, with big feet." Recalling a recent patron who had reported an injured coot and feeling this species might answer my present caller's description, I asked, "Does it look like a duck?" to which the person on the other end of the line responded emphatically, "No! It is a *bird*!" Forbearing to inquire whether a duck was not also a bird, I suggested that, the gasoline situation being what it was, perhaps she could take care of the bird herself. But she exclaimed, "You've *got* to come and get it—it is in such agony that it is crying and moaning all the time and even our dog is upset."

I knew I would have no peace of mind over the week-end if I did nothing to alleviate a bird's misery, so I invited a shut-in friend to accompany me so that she would get some benefit from the gasoline that was being burned. When we arrived at the given address, the beleaguered owners escorted us to their beautifully landscaped backyard, enclosed by a stockade fence. There I found—a very healthy, very lively, half-grown chicken with only a slight cut on its leg to

testify to its having been involved in an accident. The chick had evidently learned its lesson well or knew by instinct to practice that vitally important behavior pattern laid down by Nature for covey-type birds: "Keep churring, keep peeping; make all the noise you can so you won't stray from the rest of the brood and become separated from your mother." I explained to the finder the reason for all the "squalling and squawking" and suggested that the bird would make a good pet, but they had had all the experience they wanted with chickens. I took the little blabbermouth, cheeping and chattering all the way, to a friend who kept some poultry on an acreage. There the chick, once it molted into its adult plumage, became quite a respectable silver-laced Wyandotte hen which occasionally produced a bonus for her owner by way of an egg.

I did not always, however, have to burn my own gas in order to get my patients; frequently the finders would volunteer to bring them to me. One evening I received a call from a man asking if I would take some kind of a duck. "Where did you find it?" I asked. "It was in the bed of my truck when I came out from work," he replied. I suspected with an explanation of that kind he might be "putting me on," but I reasoned the most important thing was that he was trying to help the duck, so I told him to bring it over. At about dusk he rang my doorbell, but since he had left the duck in the truck I suggested he bring it in. The man hesitated. "Me and that duck don't get along too well," he said. "Never mind, I'll get it," I said loftily, and taking one of the sheets that had not survived Edgar's housekeeping, I went out to throw it over the duck. But when I looked into the bed of the truck I dropped my air of superiority. It was too dark to identify positively the dark little form that was bouncing around back there, but judging from the lunges it made when I reached down in its direction, it was a "mighty mouse" indeed, and I retreated to put on a pair of gloves. Once I had the bird in hand, it proved to be a rela-

248

In general, shore birds, like the terns above, are not easy to care for and should be left alone unless an extreme emergency exists.

OPPOSITE:
Plovers (top) are common shore birds.
Gulls (below) are known to frequent in-shore regions in search of food.

tively harmless opponent, but not because of any lack of intent on its part to assault anyone who attempted to handle it; its rubbery beak simply was not an effective weapon. When I got the duck into the light it proved to be a female ruddy duck, the most aggressive species of duck I was to learn later from the bird books. Knowing it was a diving duck and finding that it had no inclination to eat, I decided that if it were to survive in captivity it must be in water deep enough to submerge itself.

Where, in the average house, can water be provided deep enough to serve as a diving pool? The bathtub—where else! So into the bathtub she went, where she did indeed dive and where she also staged swimming charges when I came too close. To provide her with a choice between swimming and perching, I "sank" a plastic wastebasket in the tub, its exposed side providing a solid base to sit on. I found she spent as much time on the wastebasket as in the water, although she obviously believed her security lay in the water, as she promptly slid off her perch whenever I came too near. To give her a choice of menu I tossed in canned bean sprouts, celery tops, lettuce, and dog meal, and hoped I would be successful in "straining out" the residue when the time came to drain the tub.

Fortunately for me, "Daisy" was not destined to make her quarters in that location for long. Although she remained strong and active, it was evident she was not eating, and I called the local zoo for assistance in coping with a hunger strike. The zoo secretary informed me the zoo was interested in taking her, since they were already force-feeding another ruddy and were investigating the possibility of there being an undetected source of duck poisoning in the area. I hastened to pass my patient on to more skilled hands and spent the following evening trying to avert a plumbing stoppage when I cleared the tub so it could function again in its usual role.

While the good intentions of the truck driver with the

Due to the use of superinsecticides, raptorial birds especially have declined in number; by ingesting certain insecticides, many female raptors lay eggs which can not form hard shells.

Great care must be taken when handling raptorial birds, as they all have sharp talons and strong beaks. Shown here is a great eagle owl.

duck were immediately apparent, I was not so sure of the authenticity of another claim made on my hospitality. One evening I received a call from a woman who sounded a bit diffident as she identified herself as an attendant at the Humane Society. I understood her hesitation when she explained the nature of her call. She stated there was a man on her phone who was seeking relief from a flock of birds "in his closet" and could she put him on the line? I too sensed a "set-up" but was curious to hear the whole story; therefore, I accepted the call. In a business-like manner a youthful voice at the other end of the line stated this was no laughing matter; he had opened his closet door that evening and found a bunch of birds staring him in the face. No, he didn't know what kind they were or how they got there. Yes, he could bring them over at once. I gave him instructions for reaching my address and settled back to wait, realizing that, in view of their location, the birds must be either house sparrows or starlings. When after more than a reasonable length of time the harassed landlord failed to appear, I began to doubt his sincerity until the phone rang again. It was the Humane Society secretary, who stated that the young man was stranded in another part of town without my address. Again she put him on the line; I gave further detailed instructions and waited a second time. When 11 p.m. arrived and I still had no visitor, I was certain he was playing a joke and regretted that a person with a taste for that type of humor had my address.

I had nearly forgotten the incident by the following noon, when, in answer to the doorbell, I found two young men on my doorstep, one holding a box containing five fledgling starlings and the other a coffee cup containing, presumably, that beverage. "We finally got here with the birds," said the youth with the coffee cup. "I thought you were putting me on," I said. The lad took a gulp from his cup. "I got drunk last night," he confessed, "and couldn't find this place!" "Was it all that bad having birds in your house?" I asked. He reflected briefly, then took a second draught from his cup. "Yes it was," he stated.

The mystery of how the birds got into his closet was solved when he explained he lived in an old house converted to apartments. Some plumbing pipes ran up through his closet wall; work had been done on the plumbing recently and the holes in the wall had not been completely closed up. Obviously, a pair of starlings had gained access to the attic and made their nest somewhere above his closet. When the young were old enough to ramble about they tumbled through the holes around the pipes into the closet, where they confronted him as soon as he opened the door.

Seeking to replace this apparently harrowing memory with one more pleasant involving a bird, I invited the young men to witness Picklepuss's dance routine. Finding himself the center of attention, the cockatoo put on a good show, using a slip of paper, like a fan, to enhance his performance. I wondered afterwards, however, if in view of the youth's reaction to the starlings, I had done him any favor with this diversion. Might he, upon future reflection, equate the pink parrot with pink pachyderms and seek re-

"First he had birds in his closet, now it's pink parrots _dancing_"

Peregrine falcons are capable of diving at prey at speeds of over 170 m.p.h.

lief from his visions through another trip to the courts of Bacchus?

However, if my "customers" had difficulty finding my address, I likewise experienced difficulty at times finding addresses to which I had been called and occasionally more difficulty when I arrived. One evening I received a call to pick up an injured robin, the finders asking me to state a specific time for my arrival, which I did. However, my plans changed, and I arrived for the bird earlier than I had specified. When I reached the address I found a sign on the gate stating "Beware of the Dog." I reflected on this warning for a moment, but neither seeing nor hearing any evidence of said dog and fancying myself a Florence Nightingale of the birds who would brave any dangers to minister to a patient, I opened the gate and entered the yard. Once inside, however, I realized I had made a serious error. A large police dog arose from his place of concealment behind a bush and proceeded to demonstrate that the posted sign meant just what it said. I have always had a fear of being bitten by a dog, but I tried to avoid any sign of panic by saying "Nice doggie" as soothingly as I could under the circumstances. I didn't mean it and he knew it! After a few diversionary tactics he grabbed me at that spot dearest to the heart of all watchdogs—the seat of my pants. Fortunately, I was wearing a skirt which my mother had crocheted out of heavy woolen yarn, and the resulting mouthful kept the dog's fangs from more than scratching the "real me." Luckily, while the house on the back of the lot appeared to be deserted, the owners were at home and, hearing the commotion, came running out, explaining it was for this reason they had wanted me to be specific about my arrival time. On this occasion I did not linger long to express my usual gratitude for their kindness to the animal kingdom, feeling at that point that the animal kingdom had not been very kind to me. I took the robin and made a hurried departure. Later examination revealed that the dog's

Hootin' Harriet—a fourteen-year-old great horned owl who will eat nothing but chicken and shows a distinct preference for the white meat.

fangs had torn the crocheted fabric of the skirt. Since I lacked the skill to make repairs myself, that item of apparel went out of service, having, however, more than fulfilled any expectations my mother may have had for its future usefulness to me.

Occasionally, the foundlings themselves posed a threat to my well-being. One Saturday morning I received a call that a great horned owl had been sitting on the caller's incinerator for two days, rejecting hamburger offered it. Anxious to be rid of this omen of ill fortune, the family requested me to pick it up. I could not find my one pair of leather gloves, so I took a heavy blanket along to avoid contact with the bird's powerful beak and talons. The owl made no objection to being wrapped up in the blanket, and I placed my lethal "baby" in a cage in the back of my car and hastened home. On my arrival I found a couple of teenagers had stopped by to take a look at my birds. Although I recognized the danger inherent in the bird's natural weapons, I welcomed some assistance in getting the owl out of the small carrying cage and into my backyard cage. With the enthusiasm of youth they were glad to oblige, and the transfer was proceeding smoothly until, in my concern for the boys' hands, I got my own arm in the vicinity of the bird's feet while we were trying to get him stabilized on a wooden platform in the cage. Only one person at a time should attempt to handle such a predator and then only with leather gauntlets. My wrist brushed one of the owl's feet and, seeking to get some sort of perch between his toes, he automatically locked onto my wrist. Now I know what a rat or rabbit feels like when gripped in one of these powerful vises. It was an experience I could have done without. I knew that his reflexes were much faster than my own, and if I attempted to jerk away, my wrist would be torn severely. I told the boys to lay him on the platform and that we would have to wait until he wearied of the inactivity and decided to use his feet to move elsewhere. Unfortunately, once he was placed on the platform he gave every indication that he liked it there and would be content to spend the remainder of the day in that position. No diversion offered by the boys relaxed his grip and any movement of my own tightened it. Finally, though, he decided to make a dash for liberty, sprinted across the platform, and flopped down to the ground; at the same time the three of us made our getaway, having lost all interest in keeping him anywhere he did not choose to stay. I spent a restless night. My arm hurt; through my bedroom window I could hear Hootie hopping around on the various small cages stored in his apartment, and I felt, or imagined that I felt, an ache in my jaw which made me wonder if I was coming down with lockjaw! Fortunately, however, there were no repercussions from my encounter with Hootie's talons except a permanent scar on my wrist from one of the punctures. Upon reflection, I realized I was also lucky in another respect: The bird latched onto my wrist instead of one of the boys'. Either of the youngsters might have panicked, which would have resulted in the bird's talons being driven deeper. Since I was the responsible adult in charge, the parents of the boys would have held me to blame for the injury, and bills for any medical expenses or damage would have been filed with my casualty insurance agent.

I have since been told by zoo personnel that any raptor will release its grip if a person suddenly drops his arm or whatever part of his anatomy that has been gripped, as the bird will instinctively try to avoid falling by attempting to fly. This reaction was put to good advantage by a falconer friend who averted a potentially tragic outcome triggered when a falcon he was holding on his fist suddenly sank her beak into his upper lip. He climbed upon a chair, careful to hold the bird steady so she would not tighten her grip, and then jumped off the chair. The falcon gave a startled "gasp," momentarily opening her beak, and my friend jerked his arm away, removing his attacker to a safe distance.

Another dangerous incident occurred when I permitted a young man to hold Edgar the raven. I always keep my head back when handling any bird with a long, sharp beak, but the youth trustingly bent his head towards the struggling Edgar, who promptly "nailed" him in the mouth, causing the lad's lip to bleed profusely and possibly loosening a tooth. Once again I feared possible suit for dental treatment, but the youth departed, never to be heard from again. I realized both of us had learned a lesson: me never to permit anyone to hold my big birds, and he never to trust a bird's beak. This is a lesson anyone would do well to take to heart. Eyes, with their shiny surfaces, are natural targets for any frightened bird. I always shudder, too, when friends demonstrate their budgie's fondness for perching on the bows of their glasses. In such cases the beak is not the danger spot; it is the sharp little toenails which might accidentally scratch the surface of the eyeball, causing an infection. Birds certainly hold an important place in the lives of many people, but that place should never be in proximity to the human face.

But, in general, most of the operations involved in my bird infirmary were conducted without incident, and I made many fine acquaintances among my clientele. I found that compassion is not bounded by social or financial status, race, color, or creed. Any difference lay only in the method by which my patrons expressed their appreciation for my efforts. Some well-to-do households offered me substantial sums of money to buy bird supplies or presented me with some attractive gift. Others, no less sincerely, could offer only their thanks or, on some occasions, vegetables from their gardens, tucked away in the overgrown backyards of large, older houses.

However, in any nonprofessional bird hospital, in spite of

Probably the most familiar of all North American birds is the robin.

the good wishes of the finders and the efforts of the operators, only a small percentage of the birds referred there recover so completely that they can resume their normal lives in the wild. When they do, it is difficult, from a psychological standpoint, to release a bird on which great effort and care have been spent and for which a bond of affection has developed. To send such a bird out into the hazards imposed by Nature, compounded by the even greater dangers created by man, is always a harrowing experience. Yet Nature's law, no less than man's, requires that such birds be returned to their natural element.

I recall one summer afternoon, when a black sky and rolling thunderclaps indicated a downpour was imminent, I went out to bring in a young robin which I knew could not withstand such a soaking. As I opened the gate to enter the cage, a young dove that had regained the use of his wings and was restless suddenly launched himself with split-second timing straight for the open gate. Although I was standing in the entrance and must have represented to him a formidable obstacle, he knew that only through that portal could he escape from what had become for him a prison. He bore down upon me, nearly brushing my face with his wings as he veered past, and vanished into a stormy sky which held no promise for the future, no hope for security—only freedom.

Yes, as so often happens when a person takes off on an unknown path, the farther I went in the direction pointed by kind little Nellie the more deeply I became involved, until the course on which I had embarked only casually became a commitment, a way of life. In it I found all the elements one encounters in human experience: the exhilaration of success and the despondency of failure; interludes of rapture and periods of gloom; confrontations with danger and moments of frustration and uncertainty—and, always, the mystery of life and death. But most important of all was the satisfaction of knowing that I was responding to and nurturing in myself and in others that rarest of gifts—one of the most recent to emerge as a human trait, possessed only by man, and yet suppressed, ignored, ridiculed by large segments of the human race, but without which no human heart is truly human—compassion.

CHAPTER XX
Bird Feeding in an Eggshell

Anyone who owns a bird, even a pigeon or a parakeet, will find that he has acquired, in the eyes of the neighborhood, the status of "bird expert." Thus, when inevitably an injured or orphaned bird is found, its discoverer will wend his way to the bird expert's door with a request for information as to what to do with the bird. In most instances, the "bird person" will not have to probe very deeply to learn that what the caller really hopes for is an offer to take the bird off his hands. For this reason I have included an account of some of the menus I have used and the actions I have taken which have proven more or less successful. I emphasize that the enumeration of species and the diets recommended are far from being all-inclusive and are listed for illustrative purposes only. The reader interested in pursuing this subject further will find additional information in the publications listed in the attached bibliography.

I recount these experiences in the hope that they will prove useful to my readers in their personal efforts to extend a helping hand to the wildlife in their communities and lead to a better understanding and appreciation of the natural resources that make any neighborhood a better and more interesting place in which to live.

BABY BIRDS

Use only soft foods of the types given below.

NEVER feed bird seed to any baby bird; this is the equivalent of giving popcorn and nuts to a human infant.

Altricial Birds

ROBINS, SPARROWS, FINCHES, WOODPECKERS, SWALLOWS, ORIOLES, JAYS, FLYCATCHERS, AND MOST INSECTIVOROUS BIRDS:

The basic ingredient is dog food, either canned or soaked meal. The following can also be fed: canned cat food (other than fish base), lean hamburger, and other lean chopped meat, such as beef heart and liver. Grapes, cherries, apples, soaked raisins, soaked bread, hard-boiled egg, any available insects, earthworms (for robins), and moistened nestling food (available at pet stores).

DOVES AND PIGEONS:

Soaked dog meal mixed with dry wheat germ, baby cereal, instant oatmeal, or uncooked wheat cereal preparations (do not use rice).

"Now remember, no bird seed for Junior"

Mourning doves.

The moist mixture must be pushed into the squabs' mouths, as they do not "open up" as does a robin. Some people become adept at this operation using a straw or even an eyedropper (which, however, is likely to become clogged with solid particles). The "penclip" feeder described on another page may also be used. If none of these methods work, remember that "fingers were made before" any of man's implements. It is nearly impossible to keep the bird's "bib" from becoming soiled with the spillover. When the young are fully feathered and able to fly, they can be weaned to chick mash, chick scratch, and wild bird seed, which at that age they instinctively begin to pick up themselves. When they eat these items on their own, they are ready for release.

Precocial Birds
GALLINACEOUS ("CHICKEN-TYPE," SUCH AS QUAIL, PHEASANTS, GROUSE):
Baby chick mash, gradually working up to chick scratch and coarser poultry preparations. Do not "force-feed."

LEAVE THEM ALONE!

Keen-eyed children frequently find such chicks as this killdeer chick and bring them home. If the parents can be located, the young should be returned to them immediately. The belief that parent birds will not accept their young once they have been handled is erroneous. Most birds do not have such a keen sense of smell, and the young have a far better chance of survival if taken back to their parents.

Their instinct for pecking will lead these chicks to investigate food sources by themselves. These are not easy birds to raise, however, and should be left alone except in an extreme emergency.

267

GOSLINGS AND DUCKLINGS:

There are commercial preparations available at feed stores for raising domestic ducks and geese, and these may be used. However, with my ever-present supply of dog meal, I have used this for these young also, softening it first and then floating the pellets in the birds' drinking or bathing dish. Scraps of lettuce, whole-wheat bread, canned or frozen corn, grain sprouts. Work up to coarse chicken feed.

SHORE BIRDS (KILLDEER
MOST COMMONLY FOUND):

Extremely difficult to raise. Should never be taken except as a last resort. Place in a heated enclosure with a soft sand base, sprinkle any "live" or "wiggly" food obtainable, such as mealworms, chopped earthworms, fish food, live fairy shrimp, and be prepared to spend a great deal of time drawing the chicks' attention to the food by "pointing" at it, picking it up with tweezers, tapping the sand, etc. Skilled veterinarians, however, have often been unsuccessful in raising these chicks, and everyone should be discouraged from bringing them home just because they are "cute."

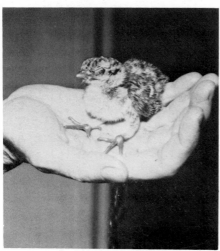

Chicks of such species as the blue grouse (left) and the killdeer (previous page) require the guidance of their parents during the first crucial days of their lives. The killdeer chick lived only because it was a week or more old before it fell into human hands and it had already learned to pick up its own food.

A yellow-shafted flicker, an insectivorous bird seen chiefly in eastern North America.

ADULTS

The common insectivorous or omnivorous birds such as robins, meadowlarks, blackbirds, jays, and woodpeckers will live indefinitely on a diet of soaked dog meal or cat food or the canned products, along with raisins and apples. The woodpeckers with which I have had experience, particularly flickers, must be force-fed on the soaked meal for several days at the outset of their captivity; otherwise they will starve to death before trying out the new diet. Some of the more exotic birds such as orioles and tanagers are fond of orange halves, from which they will "squeeze" their own orange juice.

Seed-eaters, such as finches, grosbeaks, sparrows, juncos, and other thick-billed birds, thrive on commercial bird seed, peanuts, sunflower seeds, fruits (especially apples), and some protein such as dog food or finely chopped meat. Adult doves and pigeons will live for years in captivity on the same seed mixture fed to parakeets. They will do equally well, however, on the less expensive wild bird seed and chicken feed. All seed-eaters must have gravel and mineral supplements available.

GOATSUCKERS (NIGHTHAWKS, WHIPPOORWILLS, POORWILLS):

Although these strange little creatures will live for months on a diet of soaked dog meal and finely chopped beef heart, liver, and kidney, for their own good and that of their benefactors, they should be returned as quickly as possible to their natural elements—the open sky and the night. Since they feed by snatching insects in flight, they will seldom pick up food and must be hand-fed several times a day throughout their period of captivity. Also, their small, delicate legs and feet are not meant for "heavy-duty" perching day and night and sooner or later will be broken or disjointed if these birds are confined for any period of time. The young may be successfully reared by placing small gobs of the above foodstuffs in the backs of their enormous mouths and touching the palate or placing a finger under their "chins" if they at first attempt to disgorge the unfamiliar fare. Give them abundant flying space or else confine them so that they cannot make any precipitous lunges which may result in a fall which will break a leg. Release them as soon as they have reached their full size and do well on a test flight.

Whippoorwills are not often seen because they are nocturnal.

It is illegal to keep most North American birds in captivity, but special licenses may be obtained to keep raptors in captivity.

RAPTORS (HAWKS, EAGLES, OWLS):

Both federal and state licenses obtainable only by passing a stiff examination are required to keep legally any raptor in captivity. These birds are very specialized in their dietary needs, roughage in the form of fur, bones, and feathers being essential for their continued well-being. The widely distributed sparrow hawk, or kestrel, is the member of this family that most frequently falls into human hands. I have kept a female of this species alive and healthy on a diet of beef heart, all fat removed, plus as many of the furry little beasties as I can catch at night in the outdoor cages in which I keep the seed-eating members of my infirmary. Grasshoppers feeding in vacant lots that have not been sprayed with insecticides or herbicides are an excellent source of roughage for this species if a person can catch them. A deep receptacle placed in a strategic spot in such a field will trap more hoppers than can usually be caught in a net. If the more finicky members of a family will permit it, any owner of one of these birds would do well to store as many as possible of these orthopterans in glass jars in his freezer!

271

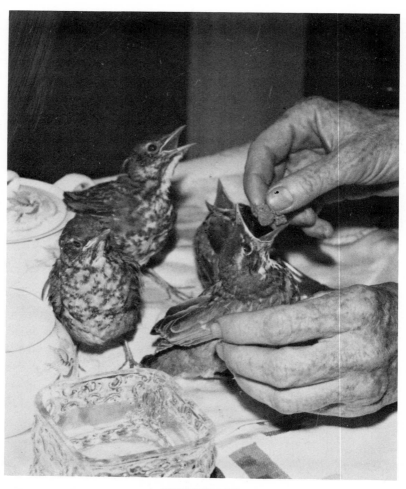

FRENCH DIP

In the natural state, altricial baby birds such as these robins get necessary moisture from their food, since the parents obviously cannot carry water to them. However, when I am feeding such birds I insure that they get their quota of both vitamins and moisture by dipping each bite into a container of water in which I have dissolved a few drops of soluble vitamins.

CHAPTER XXI

Additional Hints
for Bird Care

The above-mentioned items are by no means the only foods upon which birds will thrive, nor are they necessarily adequate to keep various birds in good health indefinitely. However, they are ingredients with which I have had success and can be obtained easily by the average person who only occasionally becomes involved in a bird-rescue effort. Individuals in even the same species may vary greatly in the way they respond to efforts to feed them; if a bird is unreceptive to one item, try another. Sometimes a bird will accept a "far-out" item. I watched in amazement as a woman shoved small pieces of baked breast of chicken into the beak of a young mourning dove she had raised, the dove swallowing them as readily as if they were standard dove fare. A friend who is very successful at raising young birds regularly prepares rice pudding and cornbread which are accepted by such unlikely diners as Bohemian waxwings and western kingbirds.

An item that is highly regarded by almost all birds is mealworms, although I am told they should be fed sparingly. These are not difficult for the average householder to raise if he has use for them in large quantities. All that is necessary is, of course, a "starter" of the worms, which may be purchased from most pet stores, and a rust-proof metal or earthen container. The "starter" should be sprinkled between alternate layers of wrapping paper or paper towels, cornmeal, oatmeal, or other dry "hot-cereal-type" breakfast foods, and a source of moisture, such as a potato

The osprey is an attractive raptorial bird which feeds on fish.

Brown pelicans are unique pelicans because they dive from the air for their dinner. Pelicans are good examples of birds whose feeding habits would make them very difficult to care for by even the most dedicated of bird caretakers and rescuers.

or apple. Newspaper, the most widely available source of paper, is not recommended for use by bird experts, since the lead in the print may be passed on through the worms to the birds themselves, resulting in lead poisoning. I had a big earthenware jar of this convenient bird appetizer available for several years, which came to an abrupt end when I rented my basement for a few months to the fiancee of my renter next door. Eager to get his beloved moved into these convenient quarters for the interim period before the wedding, the young man volunteered to clear out the accumulation stored in my downstairs kitchen. I welcomed this assistance, forgetting that my mealworm farm was also located in that room. I did not forget, however, the diplomatic manner in which the young suitor, striving to spare me embarrassment, broke the news to me that I had been harboring tenants not welcomed in fastidious households. "Oh, by the way," he stated casually, after he had made the apartment suitable for occupancy by his betrothed, "there was a crock down there in the kitchen that had some bugs in it. I just threw those out and put the crock in the storeroom." Since it was in the dead of winter I realized that my mealworm nursery had been obliterated. Since then, however, I have been able to keep my tenants healthy on a substitute diet with fewer mealworms, which I purchase from a commercial supplier.

While I doubt that anyone has ever found a satisfactory implement, other than his own fingers, for conveying a reluctant worm or other live insect prey into the mouth of a waiting fledgling, I find that the cap and clip of some types of ball-point pens is very convenient to insert lumps of soft dog food and baby cereal mixture into the mouths of such species as young finches. The clip is broad enough to hold a worthwhile amount of the mixture, and a person can use his forefinger to push it down the clip to its destination.

In addition to proper diet and frequent feedings, warmth is very important to a fledgling's survival. It is useless to at-

276

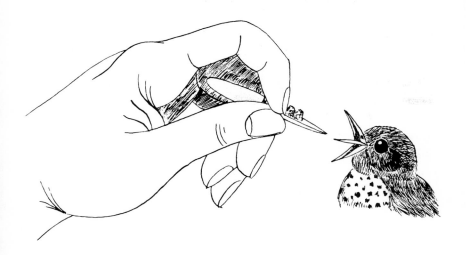

tempt to feed any bird if it is chilled, since in that stage of torpor it is unable to swallow anything. Young mourning doves, even when they are feathered out, seem to be especially susceptible to chilling. Pack such a bird in a "nest" made of a wool sock or other soft material and place it in an enclosure with a source of heat such as a light bulb (20 watts only), heating pad (turned to "low"), or a hot-water bottle filled with only medium hot water. It is important, however, not to overdo the heating, and a bird should never be left unattended in front of a hot-air register or oven.

Hand-in-hand with nutrition and temperature goes a requirement for a healthy respect for Murphy's Law, whose basic premise is: "If anything can go wrong, it will." If, as you survey your bird nursery or aviary, you can see any possible trouble spot, rest assured that sooner or later a bird will find it if you do not remedy the situation. If young birds are loose in an enclosure, a three-sided box should be placed in the entryway to "fence in" one's feet and avoid stepping on some "eager beaver" trying to be at the head of the chow line. Do not permit a crevice to exist into which a bird may slip but not be able to walk out. Never place any object where it can fall or shift position; a bird is sure to be under it when it does. Except for ducks, water must be kept in containers shallow enough to avoid drowning some imbiber. Owing to the drowning hazard, patients that can swim should be segregated from inmates that cannot. Avoid cages with sharp edges, particularly in the bottoms or the trays. Small "squirmy-type" baby birds such as sparrows or doves may slash their lower mandibles on the edges. Do not keep small hookbilled birds such as parakeets in cages with fine wire screen or mesh; if the tip of the beak gets hooked into the screen, the upper mandible may be torn loose.

Oddly enough, the name "lovebird" as applies to the genus _Agapornis_ is a misnomer in that these attractive birds are generally very aggressive birds.

When transporting high-strung adult birds such as jays, use a cardboard box, which will shut out the light and keep the bird quiet, rather than a bird cage, where, even with a cover, the bird may fight the bars and injure himself. Never leave a bird that cannot fly on a high, elevated surface. I know of a valuable parrot that broke its leg in a leap from such a height and died under the anesthetic during the subsequent operation. Because of their sensitive respiratory systems, birds are poor candidates for anesthesia, and any bird owner would be well advised to anticipate as much as possible any situation which might lead to an injury requiring extensive surgical treatment.

Finally, the person who deals with life must deal inevitably with death. Sooner or later a bird will be brought in so severely injured, sick, or paralyzed that to prolong its life can only prolong its misery. In such instances most veterinarians will administer a lethal shot for a nominal sum or even free, but these emergencies often arise on week-ends or in locations where such services are nonexistent. With small birds, ether, if available, can be applied to a piece of cotton which is then placed with the bird in a tightly closed box. I have known of people attempting to make a humane disposal of an injured bird by turning on an open gas burner, but this is obviously a dangerous practice and the bird seldom dies immediately anyway. Placing it in a box and running a hose into the box from an automobile exhaust would have been a safer solution.

I believe the quickest, most humane, and surest method is decapitation with a small hatchet. I have a sturdy board with a nailhead protruding above its surface. With small birds I tie the ends of a fifteen-inch length of thread or string together, then loop the string around the bird's neck in a slipnoose, and loop the free end over the nailhead. By drawing the bird back to the end of the string and then, gently, a little farther, I can expose the neck, the primary target, and strike a quick, clean blow that instantly releases

279

the tiny spark of life back into the great reservoir from which all life came. The string also assures that the fingers of the hand holding the bird are a safe distance from the path of the hatchet blade. Some very tiny birds, such as warblers, are difficult to hold safely even with the length of thread. I insert them in the toe of a discarded nylon stocking in which I have snipped a very small hole, working the head of the bird through the hole. I then tie a knot in the stocking behind the bird's tail, attach my thread slipnoose (string being so coarse it is likely to slip over the small heads), and, using the stocking for a handle, proceed as above. The person who disciplines himself to carry out such a swift disposal program, where called for, will be repaid many times over in peace of mind by the realization that he has discharged man's solemn obligation to the lower animals: providing humane treatment and, where necessary, a humane death to all such creatures in his custody.

But in spite of much unavoidable heartache, some members of any infirmary will prosper to the point where they are ready for release. It is at this late date that many bird rescuers, wondering whether their proteges are equipped to make their way alone, realize most fully the importance of following the basic principle which should govern all of man's wildlife rescue efforts: Never take any baby bird unless it is injured or circumstances are such that it obviously cannot survive without human intervention. A bird that has been served a manmade diet all its life is at a great disadvantage when thrown out on its own resources. Suddenly, it must find its food and stay out of reach of its natural enemies. If at all possible, a bird should be released on an acreage where there is natural cover and where someone will be available to offer food for a few days if the youngster remains in the vicinity and comes down for human aid. Young released in a fully subdivided area are in danger of meeting an untimely end from cats, dogs, and automobiles.

Although the assumption of responsibility for raising a bird to maturity is not to be taken lightly, there are rewards for the person who stands ready to give an assist to birds in true hardship cases. To watch the metamorphosis of a naked, blind lump of protoplasm whose only active feature is a gaping mouth, into an alert, inquisitive creature pulsating with life and possessed of that attribute man envies above all else in the lower animals—free, self-sustained flight—is to awaken anew to the miracle of life. And to watch such a creature as it bounds into its element on its first flight is to feel that you, too, have had a part in the act of creation, since without your personal contributions this particular miracle would have never taken place.

Canaries are small, lively birds, but they are singers, not talkers; this is a border fancy canary.

Bibliography
Bird Vocalization and Care of Cage Birds

Bates, Henry J., and Robert L. Busenbark. *Parrots and Related birds.* T.F.H. Publications, Inc., Neptune, New Jersey, 1978.

_____. *Finches and Soft-billed Birds.* T.F.H. Publication, Inc., Neptune, New Jersey, 1970.

Bronson, Julien L. *Parrot Family Birds* (including Mynahs, Starlings, Crows, and Magpies). All-Pets Magazine, Fond du Lac, Wisconsin, 1950.

_____. *Mynah Birds—As Pets.* T.F.H. Publications, Inc., Jersey City, New Jersey, 1956.

Curtis, Nancy. *Cockatiels.* T.F.H. Publications, Inc., Jersey City, New Jersey, 1963.

Duke of Bedford. *Parrots and Parrot-like Birds.* All-Pets Books, Inc., Fond du Lac, Wisconsin, 1954.

Goodwin, Derek. *Crows of the World.* "Voice and Vocal Mimicry." pp. 50-53, Comstock Publishing Associates, A Division of Cornell University Press, Ithaca, New York, 1976.

Greenewalt, Crawford H. *Bird Song: Acoustics and Physiology.* Chapter 11, "Talking Birds." pp. 166-175. Smithsonian Institution Press, City of Washington, 1968.

Lorenz, Konrad Z. *King Solomon's Ring.* Chapter 8, "The Language of Animals." pp. 83-91. Thomas Y. Crowell Co., Inc., New York, 1952.

Moon, E. L. *Experiences with My Cockatiels.* T.F.H. Publications, Inc., Jersey City, New Jersey, 1976.

Rutgers, A., and K.A. Norris. *Encyclopedia of Aviculture.* Vol. 2 and 3, Blandford Press, London, 1972.

Thielcke, Gerhard A. *Bird Sounds.* The University of Michigan Press, Ann Arbor, Michigan, 1976.

Thomson, Sir A. Landsborough. *A New Dictionary of Birds.* "Vocal Mimicry." pp. 474-476. McGraw-Hill Book Co., New York, 1964.

Thorpe, W.H. "Talking Birds and the Mode of Action of the Vocal Apparatus of Birds." *Proc. Zool. Soc.* Vol. 132, pp. 441-455, London, 1959.

Wells, Carveth and Zita. *Raff, the Jungle Bird.* Crown Publishers, 1941.

Wilmore, Sylvia Bruce. *Crows, Jays, Ravens, and Their Relatives,* T.F.H. Publications, Inc., Neptune, New Jersey, 1979.

Care of Birds

Bates, Henry, and Busenbark, Robert L. *Finches and Softbilled Birds,* T.F.H. Publications, Inc., Neptune, New Jersey, 1970.

Collett, Rosemary K., and Charlie Briggs. *Rescue and Home Care of Native Wildlife.* Hawthorn Books, Inc., New York, 1974.

Cooper, Jo. *Handfeeding Baby Birds.* T.F.H. Publications, Inc., Neptune, New Jersey, 1979.

Hickman, Mae, and Maxine Guy. *Care of the Wild Feathered & Furred, A Guide to Wildlife Handling and Care.* Unity Press, Santa Cruz, California, 1973.

McElroy, Jr., Thomas P. *The New Handbook of Attracting Birds.* Chapter XV, "Care of Young and Wounded Birds." pp. 192-200, Alfred A. Knopf, Inc., 1960.

Terres, John K. *Songbirds in Your Garden.* Thomas Y. Crowell Co., New York, 1953.

Thomas, Arline. *Bird Ambulance.* Charles Scribner's Sons, New York, 1971.

Tottenham, Katharine. *Bird Doctor.* Thomas Nelson and Sons Ltd., Edinburgh, 1961.

Yglesias, Dorothy. *The Cry of a Bird.* E. P. Dutton & Co., Inc., New York, 1962.

ILLUSTRATIONS INDEX